macromedia®
fireworks mx

training from the source

macromedia®
fireworks®mx

patti schulze

training from the source

macromedia®
PRESS

Macromedia Fireworks MX: Training from the Source

  Published by Macromedia Press, in association with Peachpit Press, a division of Pearson Education.

Macromedia Press
1249 Eighth Street
Berkeley, CA 94710
510/524-2178
510/524-2221 (fax)
Find us on the World Wide Web at:
http://www.peachpit.com
http://www.macromedia.com

Printed and bound in the United States of America

ISBN 0-201-79928-6

9 8 7 6 5 4 3 2 1

CREDITS

Author
Patti Schulze

Editor
Wendy Sharp

Copyeditor
Judy Ziajka

Production Coordinator
Myrna Vladic

Compositor
Patti Schulze

Indexer
Emily Glossbrenner

Technical Review
Mark Haynes

This edition is based upon materials developed by:
Digital Training & Designs, Inc.

Many thanks to everyone who helped me with this book: Joan Hilbert, Digital Training
& Designs, who patiently read through many iterations, and all the staff at Digital
Training & Designs, who took over as I wrote.

This book is dedicated to my Mom, who is now painting rainbows.

table of contents

Using the Eraser Tool
Using the Marquee Tools
Moving a Selection
Additional Selection Options

LESSON 2 - USING VECTOR TOOLS   44

Displaying Rulers and Guides
Using the Ellipse Tool
Using the Rectangle and Rounded Rectangle Tools
Apply Filters as Live Effects
Saving as a Style
Adding Live Effects
Using the Polygon Tool
Using the Scale Tool
Making a Copy
Rotating an Object
Using the History Panel
Masking with Paste Inside
Grouping Objects
Importing Graphics
Trimming the Canvas

LESSON 3 - WORKING WITH LAYERS   74

Using the Layers Panel
Adding and Naming Layers
Adjusting the Size and Placement of an Object
Renaming a Layer
Locking a Layer
Showing and Hiding a Layer
Picking Colors
Using the Rounded Rectangle Tool
Adding Texture and a Drop Shadow
Changing the Stacking Order on a Layer
Using Single-Layer Editing
Setting the Default Colors
Aligning Objects

LESSON 4 - ADDING TEXT 100

Adding Text
Aligning and Indenting Text
Checking Your Spelling
Importing Text
Using the Text Editor
Using the Line Tool
Using the Subselection Tool
Using Paste Attributes

LESSON 5 - ADVANCED TECHNIQUES 118

Combining Shapes
Duplicating Objects with the Repeat Command
Creating a CD
Adding a Gradient
Changing the Opacity
Adding Text Along a Path
Using the Intersect and Crop Commands
Converting Text to Paths
Applying Transformations

LESSON 6 – CREATING BUTTONS 146

Using the Button Editor
Adding a New Button
Changing Your Buttons
Adding a Name and a Link to Buttons
Importing Your Buttons
Changing Graphics to Buttons

LESSON 7 - CREATING SLICES AND HOTSPOTS

Creating an Image Map
Working with the Web Layer
Slicing an Image
Adding a Slice
Creating Disjointed Rollovers
Adding Frames
Adding a Behavior
Viewing Full Screen
Adding More Slices

LESSON 8 - OPTIMIZING AND EXPORTING

Using the Export Wizard
Choosing the Image Format
Exporting JPEG Images
Previewing in the Browser
Exporting HTML
Using the Quick Export Button

LESSON 9 - CREATING GIF ANIMATIONS

Creating an Animation
Using Onion Skinning
Sharing a Layer
Using Animation Symbols
Controlling Playback
Exporting a GIF Animation
Using the Export Preview with Animations
Applying Tweening
Tweening Effects

introduction

Macromedia Fireworks MX is a powerful design and graphics editor, and Macromedia
Dreamweaver MX is a robust visual Web page authoring tool. Used together,
Fireworks MX and Dreamweaver MX are a powerful pair of Web design tools offering a
complete Web development solution. The two programs offer integration features to
aid your workflow as you design and optimize your graphics, build your HTML pages,
and place the Web graphics on the page.

This Macromedia Training from the Source program introduces you to the major
features of Fireworks MX by guiding you step by step through the creation of several
Web pages. The book's 11 lessons begin with the bitmap tools to edit an image and
then take you though the steps of creating a logo for a fictitious company and
designing Web pages. You then add rollover buttons and export your pages as HTML
files. The last lesson covers the integration between Fireworks MX and Dreamweaver MX.
This book is not intended to teach you Dreamweaver, but you use Dreamweaver MX
in Lesson 11 to see how Fireworks MX and Dreamweaver MX work together. For
step-by-step instruction in Dreamweaver MX, see *Macromedia Dreamweaver MX:
Training from the Source*, also published by Macromedia Press.

This roughly 16-hour curriculum includes these lessons:

Lesson 1: Bitmap Editing
Lesson 2: Using Vector Tools
Lesson 3: Working with Layers
Lesson 4: Adding Text
Lesson 5: Advanced Techniques
Lesson 6: Creating Buttons
Lesson 7: Creating Slices and Hotspots
Lesson 8: Optimizing and Exporting
Lesson 9: Creating GIF Animations
Lesson 10: Masking and Pop-Up Menus
Lesson 11: Integrating with Dreamweaver MX

Each lesson begins with an overview of its contents and what you can expect to learn. Lessons are divided into focused, bite-size tasks to build your Fireworks skills. Each lesson builds on what you've learned in previous lessons.

SETTING UP THE LESSON FILES

You'll find all the files needed for these lessons on the accompanying CD. Copy the Lessons folder to your hard drive before you start the lessons.

As you work through the lessons, you will open files within the Lessons folder. If you are working on a Windows machine, the files you copy from the Lessons folder on the CD are locked. The locked files are a concern only in Lesson 11. If you do not unlock the files, you will get a warning message when you open them.

Some folder names and file names are capitalized in this book for readability. Some Web servers do not support capital letters for file names. When you are building your images and HTML pages, it is a good idea to use lowercase for all of your file names. That way, you are ensured that the file names are supported on any server.

MACROMEDIA TRAINING FROM THE SOURCE

The Macromedia Training from the Source and Advanced Training from the Source series are developed in association with Macromedia, and reviewed by product support teams. Ideal for active learners, the books in the Training from the Source series offer hands-on instruction designed to provide you with a solid grounding in the program's fundamentals.

The lessons in this book assume that you are a beginner with Fireworks but that you are familiar with the basic methods of giving commands on a Windows or Macintosh computer, such as choosing items from menus, opening and saving files, and so on. For more information on those tasks, see the documentation provided with your computer.

Finally, the instructions in the book also assume that you already have Fireworks MX and Dreamweaver MX installed on a Windows or Macintosh computer, and that your computer meets the system requirements listed on the System Requirements page.

THE TRAINING FROM THE SOURCE APPROACH AND ITS ELEMENTS

Throughout this book, you will encounter some special features:

Tips: These highlight shortcuts for performing common tasks or ways you can use your new Fireworks skills to solve common problems.

Power Tips: These highlight productivity shortcuts.

Notes: These provide background information about a feature or task.

Italic terms: Words in italic indicate the exact text or file name you need to enter in a dialog box or panel as you work through the steps in a lesson.

Menu commands and keyboard shortcuts: Alternative methods for executing commands. Menu commands are shown like this: Menu › Command › Subcommand. Keyboard shortcuts are shown like this: Ctrl+Z (Windows) or Command+Z (Macintosh). The + between the names of the keys means that you should press both keys simultaneously. Both Windows and Macintosh commands will always be included.

WHAT YOU WILL LEARN

By the end of this book, you will be able to:

- Use the bitmap tools in Fireworks to edit an image

- Use the vector tools to draw shapes

- Combine simple shapes to create complex objects

- Add text effects, such as text on a path, to your pages

- Create buttons with rollovers and use effects for realistic-looking buttons

- Optimize and export your images

- Create animated GIF images

- Use masking techniques for isolating portions of an image

- Add pop-up menus

- Use Dreamweaver MX to add text to your exported HTML pages

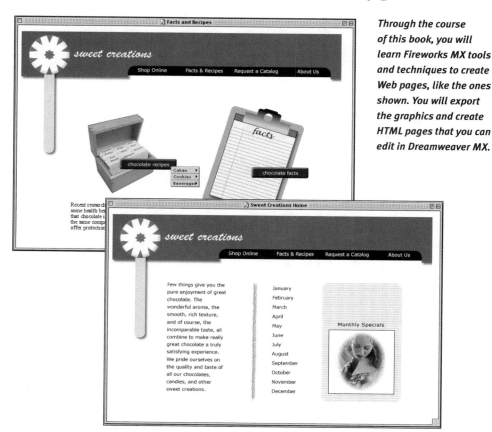

Through the course of this book, you will learn Fireworks MX tools and techniques to create Web pages, like the ones shown. You will export the graphics and create HTML pages that you can edit in Dreamweaver MX.

MINIMUM SYSTEM REQUIREMENTS

Windows

- 300 MHz Intel® Pentium® II processor
- Windows 98 SE, ME, NT® 4 (Service Pack 6), 2000, or XP
- 64 MB available RAM (128 recommended)
- 80 MB available disk space
- CD-ROM drive
- 256-color monitor with at least 800 x 600 pixel resolution
- Adobe Type Manager® version 4 or later for use with Type 1 fonts
- Version 4 or later of Netscape Navigator or Internet Explorer

Macintosh

- Power Macintosh G3 processor running OS 9.1 or later
  or OS X version 10.1 or later
- 64 MB available RAM (128 recommended)
- 80 MB available disk space
- CD-ROM drive
- 256-color monitor with at least 800 x 600 pixel resolution
- Adobe Type Manager version 4 or later for use with Type 1 fonts (OS 9.X only)
- Version 4 or later of Netscape Navigator or Internet Explorer

bitmap editing

Macromedia Fireworks MX is both a bitmap editor and a vector drawing program. By combining these drawing methods into the same application, Fireworks gives you a very powerful and versatile set of tools.

Bitmaps are images that are composed of pixels. As with paint on a canvas, you can't just remove a mistake—you need to erase or "paint" over the mistake. Vector objects are images composed of mathematical lines and therefore can be moved and reshaped or even deleted with minimal effort.

Fireworks combines the look of bitmap images with the flexibility, control, and editability of vector graphics in a single environment. You can create soft, fuzzy drop shadows on objects and then change the shape of the object, and the drop shadow is re-created for you to match the new shape.

In this lesson, you will use bitmap tools to create images for the home page in your Web site.

Editing a bitmap and manipulating a vector object are two distinct operations. The Fireworks Tools panel is divided into a set of vector tools and a set of bitmap tools to make it easy for you to choose the proper tools. If you have a bitmap image selected and you choose a vector tool, Fireworks automatically switches you to vector editing mode. If you have a vector object selected and you choose a bitmap tool, you are switched to bitmap editing mode if there is a bitmap object on the canvas. If you don't have a bitmap object, the pointer changes to the universal No symbol—a circle with a diagonal line through it— to alert you; Fireworks won't let you use a bitmap tool on a vector image. The switching is so seamless, you might not even realize that it has happened.

WHAT YOU WILL LEARN

In this lesson, you will:

- Learn the difference between bitmap and vector graphics
- Learn about the Fireworks interface
- Use the Crop tool
- Use the Info panel
- Use the Magic Wand tool
- Use the Lasso and Polygon Lasso tools and the Marquee tool
- Add and subtract selections in bitmap mode
- Scale an image
- Use the Rubber Stamp and Smudge tool

APPROXIMATE TIME

This lesson takes approximately 2 hours to complete.

LESSON FILES

Starting Files:

Lesson01\pecan_cluster_raw.png
Lesson01\toffee_ball_raw.png
Lesson01\cake_w_nuts.png
Lesson01\girl_with_candy.png
Lesson01\gift.png

Completed Projects:

Lesson01\Completed\december.png
Lesson01\Completed\september.png
Lesson01\Completed\start.png

EXPLORING THE FIREWORKS MX TOOLS PANEL

Fireworks MX has a variety of tools you can choose by clicking the tool icon on the Tools panel or by using the shortcut key shown in the following figure. If a tool has a small black triangle in the bottom right corner, it is part of a group of tools; hold down the mouse on the tool to access the pop-up tool group.

For example, hold down the mouse on the Pointer tool (top left on the Tools panel) to see the other tool (the Select Behind tool) in this group. If the Tools panel is not open, choose Window > Tools. The shortcut key for the Pointer tool is either V or 0 (zero); you can press either of these keys to cycle to the other tool in the group.

To make it easier to find the tool you need, the Tools panel is divided into six sections: Select, Bitmap, Vector, Web, Colors, and View. The tools in all of these sections are explained in the lessons in this book.

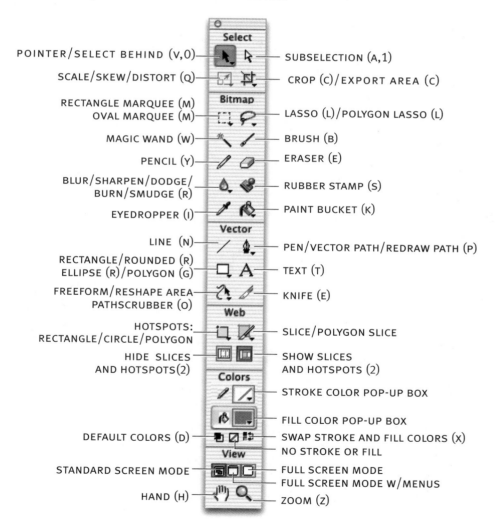

POINTER/SELECT BEHIND (V,0) — SUBSELECTION (A,1)
SCALE/SKEW/DISTORT (Q) — CROP (C)/EXPORT AREA (C)
RECTANGLE MARQUEE (M)
OVAL MARQUEE (M) — LASSO (L)/POLYGON LASSO (L)
MAGIC WAND (W) — BRUSH (B)
PENCIL (Y) — ERASER (E)
BLUR/SHARPEN/DODGE/
BURN/SMUDGE (R) — RUBBER STAMP (S)
EYEDROPPER (I) — PAINT BUCKET (K)
LINE (N) — PEN/VECTOR PATH/REDRAW PATH (P)
RECTANGLE/ROUNDED (R)
ELLIPSE (R)/POLYGON (G) — TEXT (T)
FREEFORM/RESHAPE AREA
PATHSCRUBBER (O) — KNIFE (E)
HOTSPOTS:
RECTANGLE/CIRCLE/POLYGON — SLICE/POLYGON SLICE
HIDE SLICES
AND HOTSPOTS(2) — SHOW SLICES
AND HOTSPOTS (2)
— STROKE COLOR POP-UP BOX
— FILL COLOR POP-UP BOX
DEFAULT COLORS (D) — SWAP STROKE AND FILL COLORS (X)
NO STROKE OR FILL
STANDARD SCREEN MODE — FULL SCREEN MODE
FULL SCREEN MODE W/MENUS
HAND (H) — ZOOM (Z)

FLOATING AND DOCKED PANEL GROUPS

The panels used for changing images or objects "float" above the document, so they are always on top. When you first launch Fireworks, you'll see some of the panels grouped together on the right side of the screen. You click the disclosure triangle of the panel to open or close the panel.

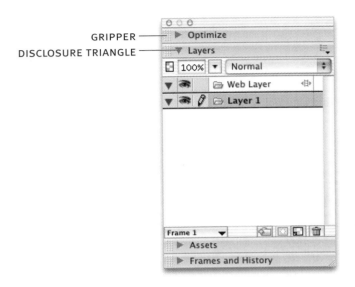

GRIPPER

DISCLOSURE TRIANGLE

Not all of the panels are initially grouped together. For example, choose Window > Swatches. A panel group named Colors opens, floating on top of your workspace. In this panel are the Swatches and Mixer panels. Click the panel tab to select it. If you want to include the Colors panel group with the other group, move the pointer over the left side of the panel, over the dotted area, called the gripper. The pointer changes to a four-pointed arrow in Windows or to a hand on the Macintosh. When you see this pointer, drag the panel to the other panel group. When you release the mouse button, the panel is docked with the other panel group. To remove a panel from the group, move the pointer over the dotted area until you see the pointer change as before; then drag the panel from the group.

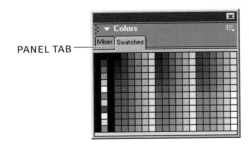

PANEL TAB

9

As you work with the panels, you'll move them around or close them. To restore the panels to their original positions, choose Commands > Panel Layout Sets and choose from one of the listed screen sizes. The panels are positioned based on the screen size you choose. This command is also handy when you change monitors—when you execute the command, the panels move to accommodate the new monitor.

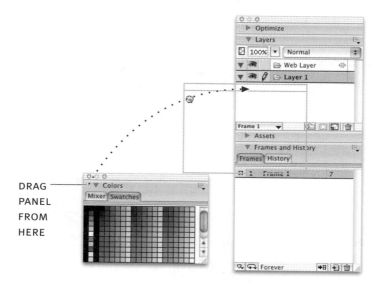

Drag a panel from the gripper and drop it within the panel docking area.

DRAG PANEL FROM HERE

THE PROPERTY INSPECTOR

The Property inspector appears by default at the bottom of your workspace. It contains information and controls for changing various values of the selected object. For example, if you have a vector object such as a rectangle selected, you can see (and change) the width and height and the X and Y positions. You can also control the fill, stroke, and effects of the rectangle in the Property inspector. Later lessons provide more information about these controls. If the Property inspector is not visible, choose Window > Properties to open it. Click the expander arrow at the lower right of the panel to minimize or maximize the panel.

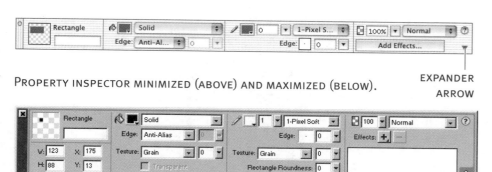

PROPERTY INSPECTOR MINIMIZED (ABOVE) AND MAXIMIZED (BELOW).

EXPANDER ARROW

EDITING BITMAP OBJECTS

Photographs or scanned art can be opened or imported into Fireworks. Fireworks recognizes the following bitmap file formats: Photoshop native files (PSD), TIFF, JPEG, GIF, BMP, PICT (Macintosh), PNG, and Targa. After you have opened or imported an image, you can make a variety of changes.

Before you can change pixels in a bitmap image, you first select the area you want to affect. After you make a selection, you can edit only those pixels within the selection. Pixels outside the selection are protected from change. This exercise introduces you to the bitmap editing tools. You will learn to make selections, change colors in the image, and clone part of the image.

When editing bitmaps in bitmap mode, you will be either editing pixel by pixel (with the Pencil, Pen, or Eraser tool) or editing a selection of pixels. Use the selection tools to select pixels either by their color values or by their location within an area. Only those pixels within the selection marquee are affected by any changes you make.

In this exercise, you will edit some bitmap images and combine them to create one image.

1) Open the pecan_cluster_raw.png file in the Lesson01 folder.

This file is a picture taken with a digital camera of a piece of candy on gray cardboard. You want to use the candy, but you want to delete the gray background.

2) Select the Pointer tool on the Tools panel and then click the candy image.

A blue border appears around the image to indicate that it is selected. The Property inspector reports that the object is a bitmap and shows its size (W and H) and its position on the canvas (X and Y). You could enter new values to resize the image in the Property inspector, but you don't need to do that for this step.

CHANGING THE VIEW MAGNIFICATION

If you have a small monitor, you may not see the blue border around the image or the entire image. There are several ways you can change the view magnification of the image in Fireworks. At the bottom of the document window, you'll see a view percentage. Click this number and select a percentage from the pop-up menu that appears.

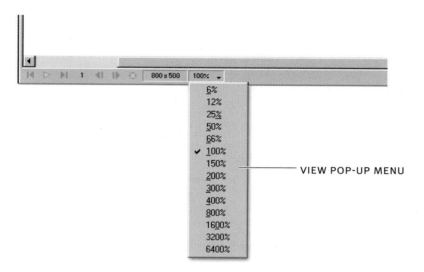

VIEW POP-UP MENU

You can also select the Zoom tool from the View section of the Tools panel. Click the canvas to zoom in or increase the view percentage. Hold down Alt (Windows) or Option (Macintosh) as you click with the tool to zoom out or decrease the view percentage.

ZOOM TOOL

The View menu includes Zoom In and Zoom Out commands as well as a Magnification submenu that you can use.

The keyboard shortcuts to zoom in are the same as in Macromedia FreeHand and Adobe Photoshop: Ctrl+Spacebar (Windows) or Command+Spacebar (Macintosh). To zoom out, use Ctrl+Alt+Spacebar (Windows) or Command+Option+Spacebar (Macintosh).

NOTE *In Windows, hold down the Spacebar first and then add Ctrl and then the Alt key. If you hold Alt down first and then the Spacebar, you access the application menu.*

TIP *Double-click the Zoom tool on the Tools panel to return the view to 100 percent.*

CHANGING THE CANVAS COLOR

The canvas color is the background color of your document. When you export an image for placement on a Web page, you generally want to make the canvas the same color as the background of your Web page so that the image blends in with the page.

For this exercise, you want to make the canvas color white to make the effects that you will add later in the lesson easier to see.

To change the canvas color, do one of the following:

- Choose Modify > Canvas > Canvas Color. In the Canvas Color dialog box, select White.
- Click the Canvas color box in the Property inspector. Choose White from the color palette.

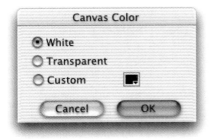

The Property inspector displays information about the selected object. If nothing is selected, then the Property inspector displays information about the document: the canvas color and canvas size. If your bitmap image is selected, switch to the Pointer tool and click outside the image to deselect it, or choose Select > Deselect. Click Canvas Size or Image Size on the Property inspector change the size of the canvas or the size of the image.

NOTE *Document settings appear in the Property inspector only if nothing is selected on the page.*

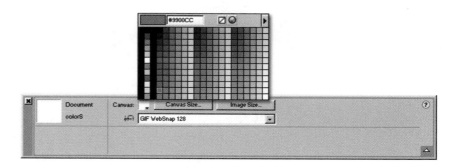

USING THE CROP TOOL

The pecan_cluster_raw.png image shows not only the candy on the gray background, but also part of the table where the image was shot. You don't need all that surrounding material—you just need the candy for the final image. The Crop tool allows you to select a rectangular portion of the image you want to keep and deletes the rest.

1) Select the Crop tool from the Tools panel.

The pointer cursor changes to the cropping tool cursor.

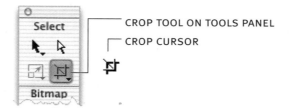

2) Start at the top left of the candy image and drag diagonally to the lower right side.

As you drag, you'll see a dashed rectangle that indicates the area you want to keep. Even after you release the mouse button, you can modify the area by dragging one of the corner handles or dragging on the sides of the rectangle. If you want to move the cropping rectangle, drag from within the rectangle to the new location. The pointer appears as a four-pointed arrow when you are within the cropping area.

3) Press Enter (Windows) or Return (Macintosh) to crop the image.

USING THE INFO PANEL

When you look at the gray background of the bitmap image, all the gray pixels appear to be similar in color. There is actually a wide variety of colors. To see the difference in the colors, you can use the Info panel.

1) Choose Window > Info.

Move the pointer around the gray background of the image and notice the change of the values in the Info panel. The Info panel displays the color and position of the pixel directly below the mouse pointer.

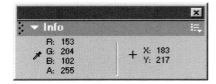

2) Click the Options menu on the Info panel and then select HSB from the menu.

The Options menu is located on the right side of all panels. This menu contains options specific to that panel. On the Info panel, you can view the hexadecimal, RGB (red, green, blue), CMY (cyan, magenta, yellow), and HSB (hue, saturation, and brightness) values of colors. When you view the HSB values, you can see the differences in gray colors that on your screen appear to be the same.

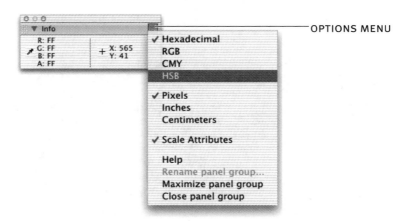

NOTE *The Options menu is common to all panels in Fireworks MX.*

USING THE MAGIC WAND TOOL

With the Magic Wand tool, you can select neighboring pixels of the same or similar color. The level of similarity depends on the tolerance level you set in the Property inspector. The lowest level, zero, selects one color; you pick the exact color with the tip of the tool. The highest setting, 255, allows the greatest range of colors to be selected. For example, if the tolerance is set to 50 and the RGB value of the color selected is R = 100, G = 100, and B = 100, then colors from 50, 50, 50 to 150, 150, 150 are within the 50 tolerance range and thus are selected.

To understand this better, look at the shades of gray in the background of the bitmap image you have open. You've already seen that the background includes a variety of shades of gray. If you use a low tolerance level, for example 10, then the gray pixels selected are limited to those in a small area around the pixel you clicked with the tool. To select the entire gray background, you need to continue to click to add pixels to the selection. If you use a large tolerance number, for example 255, then you will also select colors outside the gray color range.

1) Select the Magic Wand tool on the Tools panel.

MAGIC WAND TOOL

The Property inspector displays two options you can set for the Magic Wand tool: Tolerance and Edge.

2) Type a number in the Tolerance text box in the Property inspector or use the slider to change the value.

The tolerance level controls the number of pixels selected adjacent to the pixel you select with the tip of the Magic Wand tool. The lowest tolerance level, zero, selects only the exact pixel you selected. Increasing the tolerance level increases the number of colors in your selection. Experiment with changing the tolerance level number to see the differences in the selected area.

For this exercise, start with a tolerance of 25.

3) From the Edge pop-up menu, select Hard, Anti-alias, or Feather.

The Edge menu controls the appearance of the edges of the selected pixels. For this exercise, use an anti-alias edge for your selection.

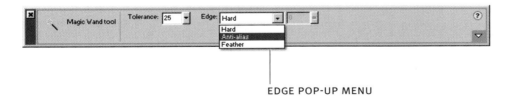

EDGE POP-UP MENU

SPRING CREEK CAMPUS

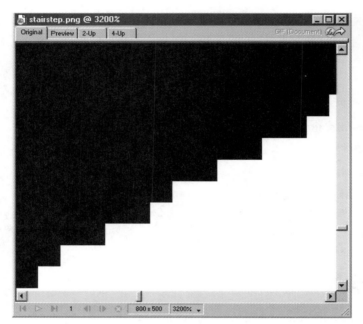

Stair-step effect on hard edge of diagonal line.

4) Click the area of the image you want to select.

Click the gray background in the image. All neighboring pixels within the specified tolerance level are selected. You should now see the "marching ants" marquee around your selection. Depending on where you initially clicked, you may not have the entire background selected.

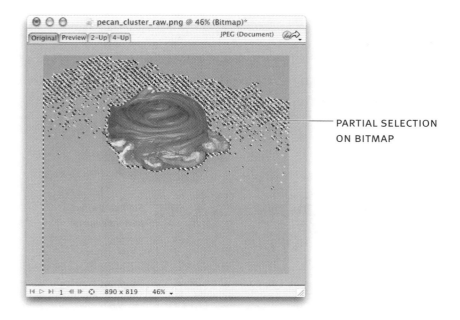

PARTIAL SELECTION
ON BITMAP

5) If you need more of the background selected, hold down Shift and click outside the boundaries of your selection with the Magic Wand to add more pixels to your selection.

Continue to hold down Shift and click until all of the background area is selected.

TIP *You can also choose Select > Select Similar to select more pixels.*

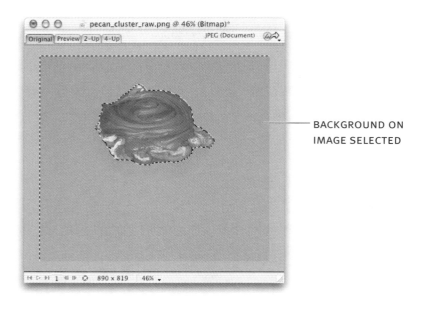

BACKGROUND ON
IMAGE SELECTED

6) Press Delete to delete the gray background.

Once the background is deleted, you'll see the white background of the canvas.

SAVING THE SELECTION

With the Magic Wand tool, you were able to select the background. If you have spent a great deal of time making your selection, you might want to save that selection so you can use it later. Once it's deselected, it is gone. But what if you want the candy selected and not the background? Since you still have the background area selected, it is a simple step to reverse the selection and get everything (the candy in this case) other than the background.

1) Choose Select > Select Inverse.

Now the selection is only around the candy. Any modifications to the image will now affect only the candy.

2) Choose Select > Save Bitmap Selection.

With the selection around the candy saved, you can later restore that selection if you need to use it again. You'll restore the selection later in this lesson.

3) Choose Select > Deselect to remove the selection.

A blue border appears around the image, indicating that you now have an object selected, not the bitmap.

NOTE *If you don't see the blue border, reduce the magnification level so you can see the outside edges of the image.*

ADJUSTING LEVELS

Occasionally you may have bitmap images where you need to adjust the color values. Perhaps the image is too dark, too light, or doesn't have enough contrast. The Levels dialog box enables you to adjust the shadows, the midtones, and the highlights of an image. For the candy image you've been working with in this lesson, you want to brighten the highlights of the pecans around the outside edges of the candy. You can do that using levels. First, you'll restore the selection you saved around the candy, and then you'll adjust the levels. You need to return to bitmap mode to restore the selection. Look at the bottom left side of the document window. If you see a red circle with a white X, you are in bitmap mode. If the circle is dimmed, you are in vector or object mode.

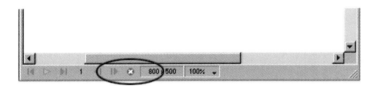

1) Select the candy with the Pointer tool.

A blue border appears around the image, indicating that you have an object selected.

2) Select one of the bitmap tools from the Tools panel; for example, select the Magic Wand tool.

The blue border around the image disappears, and the red circle with the white X is now visible. You are in bitmap mode.

3) Choose Select > Restore Bitmap Selection.

The marquee selection you saved earlier appears around the candy. Any changes you make to the image will change only the pixels within the selected area.

4) Choose Filters > Adjust Color > Levels.

The Levels dialog box displays a histogram: a plot of pixels at each lightness value. Beneath the histogram are three sliders for adjusting the black and white points and the midtones. For this image, you want to brighten the white portions of the meat of the pecans. Make sure you can see the image when you are making adjustments. You can move the Levels dialog box if you need to.

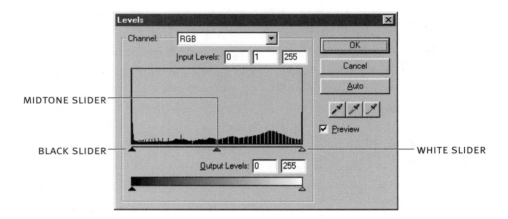

5) Slowly drag the white slider (the one on the right) to the left.

As you drag the slider, look at the light parts of the image—they get lighter the more you move the slider. You don't want the setting too light—just enough to brighten the white part of the pecans. Notice that the middle slider moves along with the right slider. The middle slider adjusts the midtones.

NOTE *Be sure to drag the white slider under the histogram, not the Output Levels slider.*

6) When you get the whites to your liking, try moving the middle slider small amounts to the right.

Notice that the chocolate part of the candy darkens when you move this slider.

7) When you are satisfied with the tonal range of the image, click OK to close the Levels dialog box. Then choose File > Save As and save this file as *pecan_cluster.png* **in the Lesson01 folder.**

VIEWING THE GAMMA SETTING

When creating graphics for the Web, how do you make the color look good on all machines? This is a nearly impossible task. Monitors are usually not calibrated accurately, nor are they calibrated the same from one machine to another. To make matters worse, on different computer platforms, shades of colors appear different.

The gamma setting on your computer affects the apparent brightness and contrast of the monitor display. The gamma setting for the Macintosh is lower than that on Windows machines. This makes images created on the Macintosh appear darker when viewed on a Windows PC. Knowing this, you have to compensate as you create your images. If you are designing on a Macintosh, create your images a little lighter; on a PC, create them a little darker.

To make your job easier, Fireworks has a built-in function for viewing the gamma setting on the other platform. If you are using Windows, choose View > Macintosh Gamma. This lightens the image to simulate its display on a Macintosh. If you are using a Macintosh, choose View > Windows Gamma. This darkens the image to simulate its display on a PC. Look at the color difference when you choose this option.

1) View the gamma setting for the alternative platform.

If you are using Windows, the image will look lighter. If you are using a Macintosh, the image will look darker.

2) Close the file.

You can close this file for now. You will use this image later in this lesson.

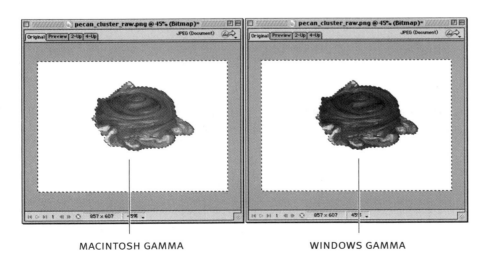

MACINTOSH GAMMA   WINDOWS GAMMA

USING THE LASSO AND POLYGON LASSO TOOLS

The Lasso tool creates a freeform selection boundary around an area. Wherever you drag, you draw a selection outline. When you release the mouse button, the selection area closes automatically. To close the selection area yourself, return to the first point of the selection. As you come close to the beginning, the pointer displays a small square. To close the selection, release the mouse when you see the square.

The Polygon Lasso tool draws straight-line segments. This tool works differently than the Lasso tool; instead of dragging the tool to make the selection, click for your first point, move to a new location, and click again to define a line segment. Just as with the Lasso tool, you'll see a small square by the pointer when you are close to the beginning point. Click when you see the square to close the selection. You can also double-click to close the selection, even if you have not moved the pointer back to the beginning point.

As with the Magic Wand tool, you can control the edges of the selection you draw with the Lasso tool. Read about this in the note in the section "Using the Magic Wand Tool" earlier in this lesson.

In the next exercise, you will select the gift in an image using the Lasso and Polygon Lasso tools. To more easily see the edges of the gift, you will want to enlarge the view. You can use the Magnification pop-up menu at the bottom of the document window or the Zoom tool. The Zoom tool enlarges the image at the point where you click.

1) Open the gift.png file in the Lesson01 folder.

This is a picture of a gift on a gray background.

2) Select the Zoom tool and click the gift.

Depending on the size of your monitor, you may want to zoom in again. You want the image large enough to show the edges of the package.

3) Select the Polygon Lasso tool from the Tools panel and change the edge setting to Anti-alias in the Property inspector.

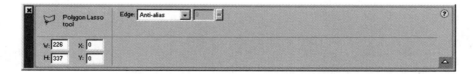

4) Click the top left corner of the package with the Polygon Lasso tool.

Move the pointer to the bottom left corner. As you move the pointer, you'll see a blue line connecting the point you clicked and the new position of the pointer. Click when you are over the bottom left corner. Continue to move and click over the remaining corners. When you run out of straight edges on the gift, double-click to close the selection area. Now you have the package selected, but not the ribbon. You'll use the Lasso tool to add the ribbon to your selection.

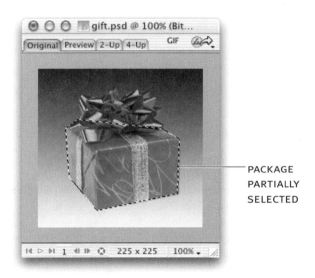

PACKAGE
PARTIALLY
SELECTED

ADDING AND SUBTRACTING SELECTIONS

Holding down Shift while you are selecting an area adds to the selection. Holding down Alt (Windows) or Option (Macintosh) subtracts from the selection. You'll use these techniques to add the ribbon to your selection of the package.

1) Select the Lasso tool. Hold down Shift and move the lasso pointer within your selection.

A plus sign appears with the lasso pointer.

NOTE *If you don't see the plus sign on the pointer and you click, your previous selection is deselected. Holding down Shift ensures that you are adding to the selection, not starting a new one.*

2) Drag the Lasso tool around the ribbon you want to include in the selection. Continue to drag around the ribbon until you return to your first selection and then move the pointer within the selection. When you are within the selection, release the mouse button and the Shift key.

The new selection is added to the previous selection.

Don't worry if your line doesn't exactly match the edge of the ribbon or if you get a wavy line. Drawing with the mouse is equivalent to drawing with a brick in your hand, and it does take some practice to draw smooth outlines. In the next steps, you'll clean up the edges of the selection you make.

3) Hold down Alt (Windows) or Option (Macintosh).

A minus sign appears with the lasso pointer. If you see areas of the selection that are outside the image, you need to delete those areas. If you see areas that you need to add to your selection, hold down the Shift key and drag around the area as you did in the previous step.

4) Drag the Lasso tool around the area you want to delete from the selection and then release the mouse button.

The area is deleted from the selection. Continue using this technique in all the areas that are outside the edge of the package.

5) Continue to add and delete areas of the selection until you have the package completely selected.

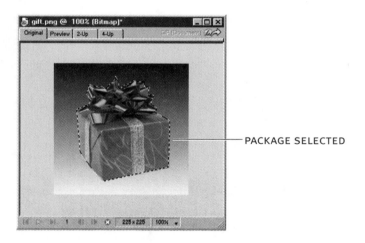

PACKAGE SELECTED

6) Choose Edit > Copy.

In the next exercise, you'll paste this copy of the package into a new document. Later in this lesson, you will create a new image by combining this package and the pecan candy that you modified earlier.

CREATING A NEW DOCUMENT

When you begin a new document, you need to set the canvas size and color and the image resolution.

1) Choose File > New to create a new empty document.

The New Document dialog box opens.

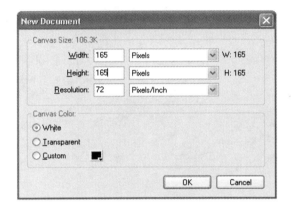

2) Set the canvas size, using pixels, inches, or centimeters. For this exercise, enter *165* Pixels for the width and *165* Pixels for the height.

You can alter the canvas size later by choosing Modify > Canvas > Canvas Size or by using the Crop tool to crop the document or by choosing Modify > Canvas > Trim Canvas to trim the empty edges of the canvas.

3) Define the resolution as either pixels per inch or pixels per centimeter. Choose a white canvas, a transparent canvas, or a custom color canvas. Then click OK.

Web graphics are saved at 72 pixels per inch by default. The resolution of the entire document can be changed by choosing Modify > Canvas > Image Size.

The canvas color is the background color of your document. (See "Changing the Canvas Color" earlier in this lesson for more information.) For this exercise, use white as the background color.

NOTE *The color you choose as the canvas color is also the color of the background page when you export to HTML. If your canvas color is set to Transparent, then the transparent background will export as a white background.*

4) Save your file in the Lesson01 folder and name it *december.png*.

In Windows, the .png extension is added automatically to your file name. On the Macintosh, select Add Filename Extension in the Save dialog box to add the .png extension. Once selected, this option becomes the default for all subsequent files you save. Although not needed for Macintosh computers, it is always a good idea to add the proper extension for your files, especially if you share files with Windows users.

NOTE *The document window displays an asterisk when you make a change to the document to remind you to save your file.*

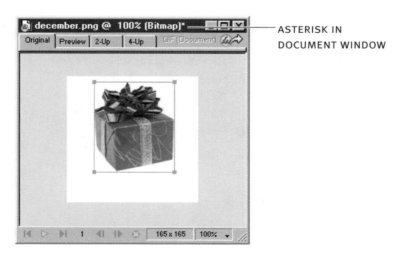

ASTERISK IN DOCUMENT WINDOW

5) Choose Edit > Paste.

The gift package you copied from the last exercise is pasted into this new document. You can close the gift.png file. You don't need to save any changes.

SCALING THE IMAGE

The package you pasted in the new document is slightly larger than the canvas, and you want to scale it down. There is a Scale tool that you can use, or you can simply drag one of the corner handles to make the image smaller. You can also precisely scale the image by a percentage.

The one thing to keep in mind is that this image is a bitmap, which means that you can make the image smaller, but you shouldn't make it larger. The resolution of the image is 72 pixels per inch, and there are not enough pixels to increase the size. If you increase the size, the image quality suffers, and you will not be happy with the resulting image.

1) Select the image with the Pointer tool.

A blue border appears around the image.

2) Select the Scale tool from the Tools panel.

Handles appear around the image and on the sides.

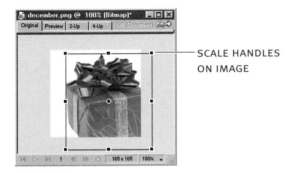

SCALE HANDLES
ON IMAGE

The Scale tool can be used both to scale and rotate an object. Move the pointer close to (but not touching) one of the corner handles. The pointer changes to a circular arrow, indicating that you are in rotating mode.

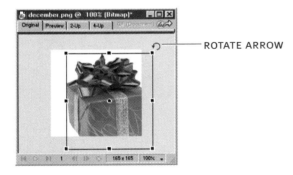

ROTATE ARROW

Move the pointer on top of one of the handles. The pointer changes to a double-ended arrow, indicating that you are in scale mode.

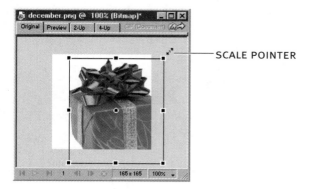

SCALE POINTER

3) Using the Scale pointer, drag the corner handle, moving it to the center. Release the mouse when the package is smaller, as shown here.

4) Press Enter (Windows) or Return (Macintosh) to release the Scale tool and change the package size. Move the package to the center of the document window.

NOTE *If you choose to drag one of the corner handles with the Pointer tool instead of the Scale tool, you need to hold down Shift as you drag to proportionally scale the image. If you don't, your image could appear distorted. With the Scale tool, you do not have to hold down Shift as you drag.*

5) Save the file.

CHANGING THE IMAGE SIZE

With the gift package complete, you now need to include the image of the candy you modified earlier. The candy image is too large to fit within the 165-by-165-pixel canvas size of the package, so you'll resize the image before combining it with the package.

1) Open the pecan_cluster.png file you created earlier in this lesson.

If there is a lot of white area around the candy, use the Crop tool to remove some of it. For this exercise, you just want the candy.

2) Select the image with the Pointer tool.

The blue border appears around the image. If you need to, decrease the view magnification so you can see all of the canvas and part of the gray surrounding document window. Look in the Property inspector. You'll see the width and the height of the image. As stated before, you could change the image size by typing new values in the Width and Height text boxes. The problem there is that to keep the image proportional, you'd need to calculate the correct values to enter. Let's let Fireworks do the math.

3) Click outside the image to deselect it.

You can click the gray portion of the document window to deselect the image. The Property inspector changes to display the document properties.

4) Click Image Size in the Property inspector.

The Image Size dialog box opens. The size of the image is displayed in pixels and inches. Confirm that Constrain Proportions and Resample Image are selected.

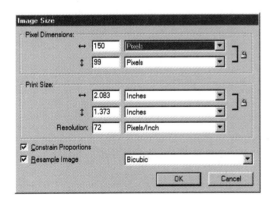

Selecting Constrain Proportions maintains the same ratio between the document's width and height. When you select Resample Image, Fireworks adds or removes pixels in the image to approximate the image at the different size.

5) Type *150* in the Width text box in the Pixel Dimensions section.

When you enter a value in one area, the other value is calculated to ensure that the image size remains proportional. This happens because Constrain Proportions is selected.

6) Click OK.

The image is resized. Position and size the document window so you can see both the gift file and the candy file.

7) With the Pointer tool, drag the candy on top of the package in the other file.

You may need to use the Scale tool to make the candy smaller so it looks proportional to the package.

COPYING THE SELECTION

The next step is to make another copy of the candy. There are several ways to make copies of your selection. You are probably familiar with the Copy and Paste commands on the Edit menu. You can use those commands, but there is a better method for controlling the placement of the copy.

32

1) Select the Pointer tool from the Tools panel, hold down Alt (Windows) or Option (Macintosh), and then drag the candy selection to a new location.

The pointer adds a plus sign, indicating that you are making a copy of the candy. Release the mouse when you are done.

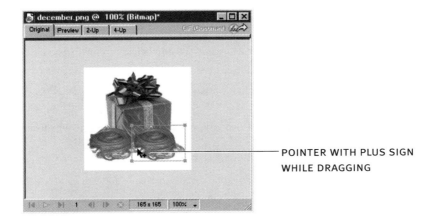

POINTER WITH PLUS SIGN
WHILE DRAGGING

2) Save the file.

ON YOUR OWN

Practice what you've just learned on the file toffee_ball_raw.png in the Lesson01 folder. Delete the gray background, resize the image, and copy the new image into the december.png file as you did with the pecan_cluster.png file. The final december.png file should look like the picture shown here. When you are finished, you can save and close the file.

USING THE RUBBER STAMP TOOL

You have a product shot of a chocolate cake with nuts, but you decide to feature the cake on your Web site without nuts. Instead of reshooting, you decide to use the existing image. You'll use the Rubber Stamp tool to remove the nuts from the cake. The Rubber Stamp tool works well for retouching an image or for cloning a portion of an image.

When you use the Rubber Stamp tool, you are painting a pixel copy of some area of a bitmap image onto another area of the same bitmap object. In this exercise, you will clone parts of the cake without nuts to cover the rest of the cake.

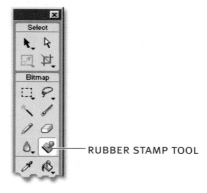

RUBBER STAMP TOOL

1) Open the cake_w_nuts.png file in the Lesson01 folder.

This file contains an image of a chocolate cake with nuts arranged on the top. To make it easier to see the nuts, zoom in on the cake with the Zoom tool, or change the View Magnification to 200 percent.

2) Select the Rubber Stamp tool on the Tools panel. In the Property inspector, set the stamp size and edge softness of the area you want to clone.

For this exercise, set the stamp size to 8 and drag the Edge Softness slider to 70. A softer edge to the Rubber Stamp tool blends your changes with the surrounding pixels. If you decide that the stamp size is too large or small, you can adjust the size as you use the tool.

3) Move the pointer to an area of the cake without a nut. Hold down Alt (Windows) or Option (Macintosh) and click to designate the set point—the point from which you will begin cloning the chocolate icing.

A circle appears to indicate your set point. The set point is the starting point of your copy. Remember using a compass in school to draw circles? At one end of a compass is a pencil; at the other end is a sharp point. You place the sharp end at a location on your paper and then drag the pencil around to draw the circle. The sharp end is the set point. The pencil is set at a fixed distance from the set point.

To use the Rubber Stamp tool, you designate the set point and then move the Rubber Stamp pointer to the location where you want to place the copy. The distance from the Rubber Stamp pointer and the set point remains constant, like the distance in the compass. As you move the Rubber Stamp pointer, the set point moves with it, keeping the distance constant. The digital information from the set point is copied and painted in the new location.

4) Move the Rubber Stamp pointer to an area with a nut. Drag to paint the area with the plain icing.

The set point moves within the icing area as you move the pointer. Continue to paint until you paint over the nut.

Repeat this process, moving the set point to a new location and painting over the remaining nuts on the cake. You'll find that the icing is not the same color over all the cake. If you use a set point too far from the nut you are trying to cover, the chocolate color may look out of place. Try to start as close as you can to the area you want to retouch.

The Property inspector provides other ways to control the behavior of the Rubber Stamp tool. Select Source Aligned when you want to release the mouse without losing the relationship to your original cloned area. This option is useful when you want to copy a portion of the image to a new location. When you release the mouse button and click another portion of the image, the distance between the set point and where you click again remains the same. Again, think of the compass example. If you leave the distance fixed between the sharp end and the pencil, you can pick up and move the set point to draw in a new location.

Deselect Source Aligned when you want to make multiple copies of the cloned area. When you release the mouse and move to a new location, the set point returns to the original position. Using the compass example again, after you complete one copy, you can increase or decrease the distance between the sharp end and the pencil, but you always begin your drawing at the same point.

The options on the Sample pop-up menu determine what portion of the document is to be cloned. If all you have in your document is a bitmap image, this setting doesn't apply. If you have vector objects along with the bitmap image, you can choose Image to clone only the pixels in the image, even if a vector object is on top of the bitmap. To copy the vector object as well as the bitmap image, choose Document.

5) Choose File > Save As and rename this document *september.png*.

USING THE SMUDGE TOOL

After using the Rubber Stamp tool to "erase" the nuts on the cake, you may notice some rough areas where you used the tool. You can use either the Smudge or Blur tool to smooth the edges. The Smudge tool smears adjacent pixel colors. Imagine two colors of wet paint on a wall. If you drag your finger from one color of paint to the other, the first color of paint blends into the other color. The harder you press on the paint, the more color is smeared into the other color. The Smudge tool works the same with pixels—you can click and drag to smear one color area into another. You have pressure, edge softness, and size controls to aid you in fine-tuning the image.

Using your september.png file, you will use the Smudge tool to smooth the icing on the cake.

1) Choose the Smudge tool from the Tools panel.

Hold down on the Blur tool to see the other tools in this tool group. The tools in this group are Blur, Sharpen, Dodge, Burn, and Smudge. You might want to set your document magnification to 200% to make it easier to see the details in the image as you use this tool.

2) Change the settings for the tool in the Property inspector. For example, change the size to *10*, the edge softness to *30*, and the pressure to *15*.

You may need to adjust these settings as you use the tool on your image. The higher the Pressure setting, the more the color is blended into the new area.

3) Drag in the areas of the image you want to smooth.

Look for areas of the icing that contain different colors and drag in those areas. Just as you would use a knife to smooth icing on a cake, you can use the Smudge tool to blend the pixels in the image. The icing doesn't need to be one continuous color. Try making swirling motions, just as you would if you were icing a cake.

You might want to experiment with the Blur tool on your image if you notice hard edges after using the Clone or Smudge tool. The Blur tool decreases the contrast between neighboring pixels. As with the Smudge tool, you can control the size and softness of the tool as well as the intensity of blur on the image. You set these controls in the Property inspector after selecting the tool from the Tools panel.

4) Save your file.

USING THE ERASER TOOL

You can use the Eraser tool in bitmap mode to delete pixels or change their color. Options for the Eraser tool in the Property inspector let you do the following.

- Use the Size slider or type a number to change the size of the Eraser tool.
- Use the Edge Softness slider to change the softness of the edge of the Eraser tool.
- Select either a circle or square for the shape of the tool.
- Use the Opacity slider to control the transparency value of the tool.

USING THE MARQUEE TOOLS

The Rectangle Marquee and Oval Marquee tools let you select specific shapes in an image. To control the size and proportions of the selections of the tool, use the Style pop-up menu in the Property inspector and choose Normal, Fixed Ratio, or Fixed Size. For Fixed Size, type the exact width and height in pixels for the selection. For Fixed Ratio, type the proportion of width to height before making the selection. You can also change the appearance of the edges of the selection. Read about this in the note in the section "Using the Magic Wand Tool" earlier in this lesson.

In the next exercise, you will select a portion of an image with the Oval Marquee tool. You will also apply a feathered (soft blur) edge to the selection instead of the default hard edge. First, you will feather the selection, and then you will delete the background.

1) Open the girl_with_candy.png file in the Lesson01 folder.

2) Select the Oval Marquee tool on the Tools panel.

3) Change the edge of the tool to Feather in the Property inspector and move the Amount slider to *25*.

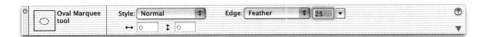

The feather amount determines the softness of the edge around the selection. You need to set the edge and the amount before you make your selection.

4) Hold down Alt (Windows) or Option (Macintosh) to draw the selection from the center outward.

Click the girl's mouth and then hold down Alt (Windows) or Option (Macintosh) and drag. The marquee selection is drawn from the center, where you clicked the image. Continue to drag until the oval selection surrounds the girl's face and part of the box of candy. You'll use the selection in the next exercise.

To constrain your selection to a circle, add Shift as you drag. For this exercise, you want an oval shape, so you don't need to add Shift.

⊙ **POWER TIP** *When using modifier keys (Option, Alt, Shift) to constrain your selection, make sure you begin to drag with the selection tool before you press the additional keys.*

MOVING A SELECTION

After you make a selection, you may want to move it to another portion of the image. For example, in the selection you just made, if you want to include more of the girl's head, you can just move the selection instead of deselecting and then re-creating the selection.

1) Create a selection with any of the selection tools.

You can use the oval selection of the girl with the candy you created in the preceding exercise.

N O T E *If you want to change the shape of your selection, you might find it easier to deselect the selection and start over. Choose Select > Deselect and make the selection again.*

2) Move the pointer within the selection.

The pointer appears as a triangle with a small rectangle below it.

N O T E *Make sure you release any modifier keys you were pressing to make the selection. In addition, don't switch to the Pointer tool to move your selection. The Pointer tool moves the image and the selection, not just the selection.*

3) Drag when you see the pointer to move the selection.

Dragging with the triangle pointer moves just the selection outline, not the pixels within the selection.

Once you have the selection where you want it, you need to reverse your selection, so you can delete the background.

4) Choose Select > Select Inverse.

This selects all of the pixels that are not in the selection.

5) Press Delete.

The background is deleted, and you see a soft-feathered edge around the girl and the candy.

6) Click the red circle with the white X at the bottom of the document window.

This exits bitmap mode and releases the selection. You could have also chosen Select > Deselect or pressed Esc.

7) Create a new document with a size of 165 by 165 pixels and a canvas color of white. Drag the modified girl image to this new document and save the file as *start.png*.

If the girl image appears too large for the new document, use the Scale tool to reduce the image to fit within the canvas size.

ADDITIONAL SELECTION OPTIONS

You can also use menu commands to make or change your selections. These commands are found on the Select menu.

Select All: In bitmap mode, selects all of the pixels in a bitmap object on a selected layer. In vector mode, selects all visible objects on all layers. If single-layer editing is on, Select All selects only objects on the current layer. Single-layer editing is covered in Lesson 3.

Deselect: Removes the selection marquee.

Superselect: Selects an object's entire group when one object in the group has already been selected. Grouping, discussed in the next lesson, binds multiple objects together.

Subselect: Selects all of the objects individually within a group selected by the Pointer tool.

Select Similar: Within a single bitmap object, creates an additional selection around colors that are similar to colors in the existing selection. The Magic Wand tool (and, thereafter, Select Similar) can also select transparent pixels or the space outside of a bitmap object as defined by the tolerance setting for the Magic Wand tool.

Select Inverse: Selects all pixels not in the current selection and deselects the currently selected pixels.

Feather: Feathers the edges of the selection.

Expand Marquee: Expands the selection by a set number of pixels.

Contract Marquee: Contracts the selection by a set number of pixels.

Border Marquee: Creates a selection outside the current selection using a set number of pixels. This selection can be filled with a color to create a border around the original selection.

Smooth Marquee: Smoothes the selection by a set number of pixels.

Save Bitmap Selection: Remembers the current selection within the document.

Restore Bitmap Selection: Restores the last-saved selection.

WHAT YOU HAVE LEARNED

In this lesson, you have:

- Examined the tools and panels [pages 9–10]
- Used the Crop tool [page 14–15]
- Used the Magic Wand tool to select pixels based on color [pages 16–19]
- Changed the hue, levels, and lightness of a selected area [pages 21–22]
- Viewed the gamma setting of an image [page 23]
- Used the Lasso tool to draw a selection around an object and then added and deleted from the selection [pages 24–26]
- Copied a selection and then moved the selection [pages 27–28]
- Used the Rubber Stamp tool to clone an area of an image [pages 34–36]
- Selected an area with the Marquee tool and then feathered the edges [pages 38–41]

using vector tools

In Lesson 1, you worked with bitmap images and manipulated pixels. In this lesson, you will work with the vector tools to create a logo for the Web site you are creating. Many objects can be created by drawing simple shapes and then combining them to create new shapes. You will learn methods to help you create a complex image from basic drawing tools. Because you are using vector tools, you will be able to easily move or change the shape of the objects you draw.

Example of the logo you will draw in this lesson.

WHAT YOU WILL LEARN

In this lesson, you will:

- Use guides for placing and aligning objects
- Draw with the Ellipse and Polygon tools
- Add Live Effects
- Scale objects
- Rotate an object
- Use the History panel to replay actions
- Mask an object using Paste Inside
- Group objects
- Import graphics
- Trim the canvas

APPROXIMATE TIME

This lesson takes approximately 2 hours to complete.

LESSON FILES

Media Files:

Lesson02\Media\sweet_creations.fh10

Starting Files:

Lesson02\None

Completed Projects:

*Lesson02\Completed\
    sweet_creations_logo.png*

DISPLAYING RULERS AND GUIDES

Guides are lines you can use to set the placement of objects on the canvas. For example, guides are helpful for aligning buttons or positioning the center point of an object. In this exercise, you'll use the guides to draw a circle for the logo. The guides will mark the center point of the circle.

1) Begin by creating a new document. Set the canvas size to _400 pixels_ for the width and height and make the canvas color white.

You can alter the canvas size later by choosing Modify > Canvas > Canvas Size, or by using the Crop tool to crop the document, or by choosing Modify > Canvas > Trim Canvas to trim the empty edges of the canvas.

⊙ **POWER TIP** _There is another way to change the canvas size. Make sure nothing is selected and then click Canvas Size in the Property inspector._

2) Save your file in the Lesson02 folder and name it _sweet_creations_logo.png_.

The page rulers must be visible for you to access the guides. If you don't see the page rulers, choose View > Rulers. A check next to the command indicates that the rulers are turned on. To hide the rulers, choose the command again to remove the check.

3) Drag from the top ruler to place a horizontal guide centered between the top and bottom edges of the canvas.

As you drag, you'll see a green line (the guide) move on the canvas. Release the mouse when you are at the center of the canvas. Don't worry about the exact placement of the ruler guide since you will adjust it in a later step.

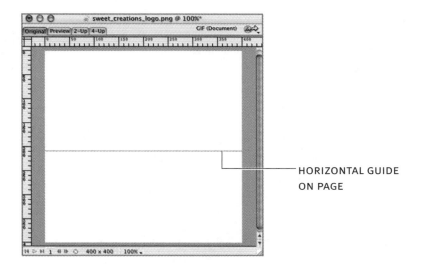

HORIZONTAL GUIDE
ON PAGE

4) Drag another guide from the left ruler to place a vertical guide on the page.

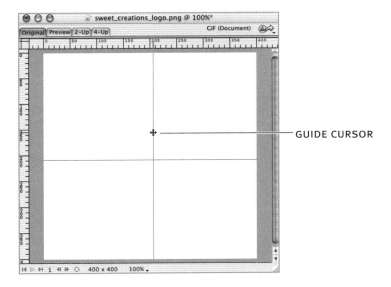

GUIDE CURSOR

5) Select the horizontal guide by double-clicking it with the Pointer tool. In the Move Guide dialog box that opens, type *200*. Then click OK.

When you drag a guide from the rulers, you are visually placing the guide on the page. When you enter a value in the Move Guide dialog box, you are moving the guide to a set position (in pixels) on the canvas.

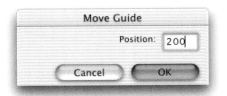

NOTE *To drag a guide from the rulers, you can have any tool selected from the Tools panel. When you move the tool pointer over the rulers, it changes to the pointer cursor. To select or move a guide on the canvas, you need to switch to the Pointer tool. The same is true for selecting objects on the canvas—you need to use the Pointer tool.*

6) Repeat the previous step for the vertical guide. Enter *150* in the Move Guide dialog box for this guide.

You can also move a guide by dragging it to a new location. When you move the pointer over a guide, it changes to indicate that you have the guide and not another object. This works only if the guides are not locked (see the next step).

To remove a guide from the canvas, just drag it out of the canvas area.

7) Choose View > Guides > Lock Guides.

You may want to lock the guides or rulers to avoid moving them inadvertently. You can also use the Guides dialog box to lock the guides. Choose View > Guides > Edit Guides to open the Guides dialog box (Windows) or the Grids and Guides dialog box (Macintosh). Here you can change the color of the guides, show or hide guides, turn Snap to Guides on or off, lock the guides, and clear all of the guides from the page. You can also change the color of slice guides (slices are discussed in Lesson 7) and show or hide the slice guides.

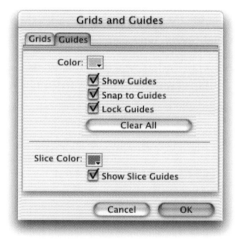

NOTE *Double-clicking a guide does not open the Move Guide dialog box if the guides are locked.*

USING THE ELLIPSE TOOL

Now you are ready to begin drawing the logo. The logo is an image of a mint candy with a design in the middle and the company name: Sweet Creations. In the next steps, you will create the candy, add an effect to make it appear three-dimensional, and add the company name to the logo. It might be useful to have a mint candy (a round white candy with red stripes around the edge) in front of you as you complete these steps. Try not to pop it into your mouth until you're finished with the logo!

1) Choose the Ellipse tool on the Tools panel.

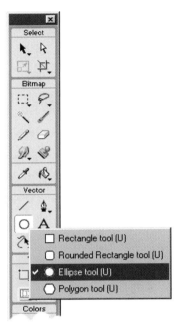

The Rectangle tool, Rounded Rectangle tool, Ellipse tool, and Polygon tool are in the same tool group. Hold down the mouse to access the tool pop-up menu and select the Ellipse tool. You'll use the Ellipse tool to draw the basic shape of the mint.

The ellipse you will draw needs to be stroked and filled with white. Strokes (the line around an object) and fills (the color or pattern within the object) are controlled in the Property inspector. If you don't see the Property inspector at the bottom of the screen (the default location), choose Window > Properties. Because so many settings are located in this panel, you'll want to keep it open as you create and edit your documents. If you have a small monitor, you can reduce or enlarge the size of the panel by clicking the size triangle located at the bottom right of the panel. In Windows, you can also use the panel Options menu located at the top right of the panel to either collapse or expand the panel.

2) In the Property inspector, choose Solid from the Fill category pop-up menu. Click the Fill color box and choose white from the pop-up color palette.

When the color pop-up window opens, the pointer changes to an eyedropper. Move the eyedropper over the color in the window to pick the color you want. When you are over a color, the top row of the window displays the color, plus the numeric value of the color. Click to choose the color.

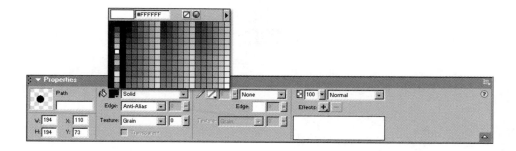

TIP *You can move the eyedropper over a color on the canvas to pick a color from an existing image or graphic. This is very handy when you want several objects to have the same color. You can also pick a color from outside the Fireworks environment. In Windows, hold down the mouse button and drag the eyedropper to the color; then release to pick the color. On the Macintosh, you can just pick any color on the screen.*

50

3) In the Property inspector, click the Stroke color box and choose a red color from the color pop-up window. For this exercise, choose the red color with the value #CC0000. From the Stroke category pop-up box, choose Pencil > 1-Pixel Soft and enter _1_ in the Tip Size text box.

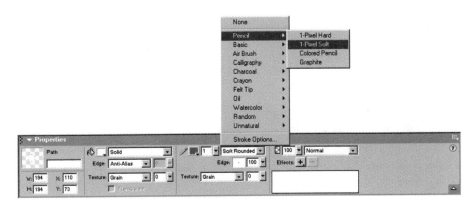

NOTE *To remove a stroke or fill, choose None from its category pop-up menu in the Property inspector.*

4) Position the cursor where the guides cross. Hold down Alt (Windows) or Option (Macintosh) to draw a circle from the center; then, as you are dragging, add Shift to constrain the shape to a circle.

TIP *Release the mouse button before you release the modifier keys; otherwise, you'll get an ellipse instead of a circle.*

NOTE *When you move over a guide, the Ellipse tool pointer turns magenta. The magenta color does not appear on the Macintosh. Macintosh users: Try setting your preferences to use precise cursors to change the pointer to red when you are over a guide. Choose Edit > Preferences; then choose Editing from the Category pop-up menu and select Precise Cursors. If you are using Mac OS X, choose Preferences from the Fireworks MX application menu.*

5) Enter _150_ for the width and _150_ for the height of the circle in the Property inspector.

With the circle still selected, look in the Property inspector. If you have collapsed the panel, expand it so you can see all of its contents. The width and height of the circle along with its position on the page are displayed on the left side of the panel. You can enter new values or just view the information. Verify that the width value and the height value are the same to ensure that you have a circle.

USING THE RECTANGLE AND ROUNDED RECTANGLE TOOLS

The Rounded Rectangle tool draws rectangles with rounded corners, the Rectangle tool draws rectangles with square corners. To change the roundness of the corners, you use the Rectangle Roundness setting on the Property inspector. You can change the roundness of rectangles no matter which rectangle tool you use. As you did with the Ellipse tool, you hold down Shift to draw a square and you hold down Alt (Windows) or Option (Macintosh) to draw a rectangle (or square if you add Shift) from the center.

ADDING LIVE EFFECTS

Live Effects are rendered effects or filters that apply to vector, bitmap, and text objects. Applying a Live Effect does not permanently change the original object—the object and the effect remain editable. If you make a change to the original object, the Live Effects change accordingly. For example, you can create a button with a bevel and a drop shadow. You can then change the color, the size, or the shape of the button, and the effects are reapplied to the new button. One or more effects can be added to an object. The effects can also be saved for use on other objects in the current document.

To make the mint appear more realistic, you'll add a bevel edge to the circle.

1) With the circle still selected, click the Add Effects button in the Property inspector. Choose Bevel and Emboss from the Effects pop-up menu and then choose Inner Bevel from the submenu.

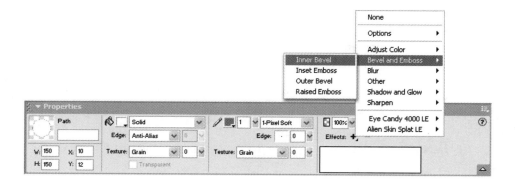

2) Change the settings to get the desired bevel effect.

Change the edge shape to Smooth in the Bevel Edge Shape pop-up menu. Drag the Width slider to control the width of the bevel. You can also control the Contrast, Softness, and Angle of the bevel. Adjust the settings to your liking.

BEVEL EDGE SHAPE
POP-UP MENU

3) Click outside the settings window to close it.

The Property inspector displays the first effect you have set for the object. You can apply multiple effects to an object by selecting other effects from the Effects pop-up menu.

TIP *When an object is selected, a blue border appears around it. In this step, the blue border is distracting, making it harder to view the beveled edge. Select the Pointer tool on the Tools panel and click outside the circle to deselect it. You might also want to hide the ruler guides. Choose View > Guides > Show Guides. This command is a toggle to show or hide the guides. Remember to select the object again if you want to make changes.*

To change your effect, click the Info icon next to the effect you want to change, or double-click the effect name in the list.

When multiple effects are applied to an object, the order of the effects in the Live Effects list can change the look of the image. Effects that change the interior of an object (such as Inner Bevel) should appear before effects that control the outer edge (such as Outer Bevel).

To reorder effects, select the effect name from the list and then drag it up or down.

To delete an effect, select the effect in the Live Effects list in the Property inspector and then click the minus button. To disable (not delete) the effect, click the check to the left of the effect in the list. Click again to redisplay the effect.

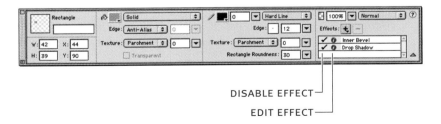

DISABLE EFFECT
EDIT EFFECT

APPLYING FILTERS AS LIVE EFFECTS

In Lesson 1, you applied a filter to a bitmap image. When you apply a filter to a bitmap object, you are permanently changing the pixel values. If you do not like the results of adding the filter, you can undo your changes by choosing Edit > Undo. Once you save the file, you can't remove the effects of the filter.

You can apply a filter as a Live Effect. Filters applied as Live Effects can be edited or removed at any time. You can apply filters to selected pixels in the image, but you can apply a Live Effect only to the entire object.

To apply a filter as a Live Effect, select the bitmap object with the Pointer tool. If you are in bitmap mode, click the red circle with the white X at the bottom of the document window to exit the bitmap editing mode; then select the object with the Pointer tool. Then choose the filter from the Effects pop-up menu.

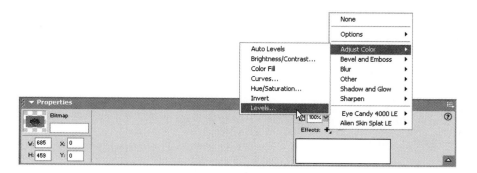

SAVING AS A STYLE

If you find yourself using the same settings or combination of effects, you can save the set.

1) Select the object with the effects you want to save. Click the plus button and choose Options from the Effects pop-up menu and then choose Save As Style.

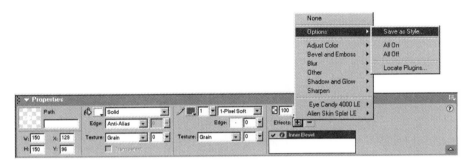

2) Type a name for the style in the New Style dialog box and then click OK.

The name of your saved effect now appears in the Effects pop-up menu. To apply a saved effect to another object, select the object and then choose the saved effect from the Effects pop-up menu.

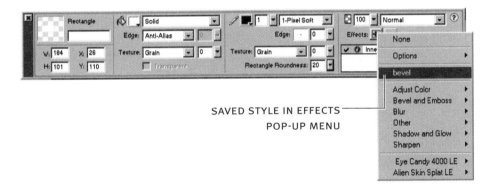

SAVED STYLE IN EFFECTS
POP-UP MENU

The effects styles you save are listed on the Styles panel, which is in the Assets panel group. Click the expander arrow on the Assets panel group if it is not open and then click the Styles tab. The style you just added is at the bottom of the panel.

You are not limited to saving effects; you can also save fills, strokes, and text styles. To save a fill and stroke of a selected object, choose New Style from the Styles panel Options menu. Name the style, and the style is added to the panel.

To delete a style, select the icon of the style on the panel and then choose Delete Styles from the Options menu.

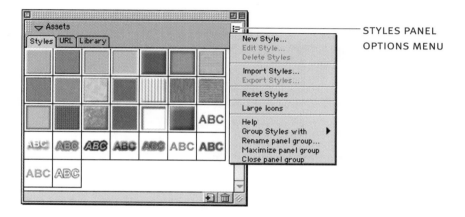

STYLES PANEL
OPTIONS MENU

USING THE POLYGON TOOL

The next step in creating the mint for the logo is to add the red stripes around the edge. If you have one of these candies in front of you, you'll notice that the red edges are really small triangles. You'll use the Polygon tool to draw one of the triangles.

1) Choose the Polygon tool on the Tools panel.

With the Polygon tool, you can draw any equilateral polygon (all sides are equal in length), from a triangle to a 360-sided polygon. With the Star option of the Polygon tool, you can draw stars with 3 to 360 points and a full range of point angles.

2) Select Polygon from the Shape pop-up menu in the Property inspector and enter *3* for the number of sides. Automatic should be checked.

If your guides are not visible, turn them on again by choosing View > Guides > Show Guides.

3) Draw a triangle on the canvas.

You want the triangle placed on the top part of the circle with one of the points (a vertex) pointing down. Position the cursor on the vertical guide at the top of the circle. Hold down Shift and drag downward. This draws the triangle with one vertex pointing down. If you don't hold down Shift, you will need to move the mouse around to get the vertex placement correct.

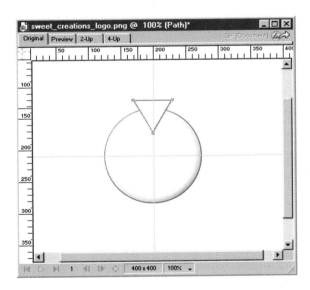

4) Fill the triangle with the same red color you used for the stroke of the circle.

You can use the Tools panel or the Property inspector to change the color. Click the Fill Color box and choose red (#CC0000) from the color pop-up window.

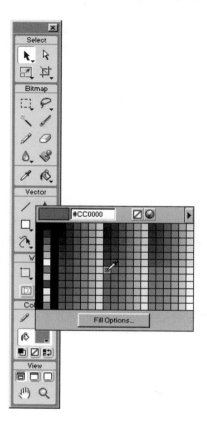

USING THE SCALE TOOL

The Scale tool can be used both to scale and rotate an object. With the Scale tool, you can proportionally scale an object, or you can distort the object by dragging a handle on one of the sides.

1) With the triangle still selected, choose the Scale tool on the Tools panel.

Handles appear around the triangle.

Move the pointer close to (but not touching) one of the corner handles. The pointer changes to a circular arrow, indicating that you are in rotating mode.

Move the pointer on top of one of the handles. The cursor changes to a double-ended arrow, indicating that you are in scale mode.

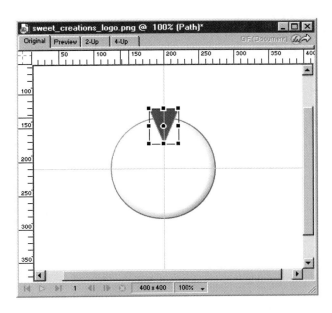

2) Using the Scale cursor, drag one of the handles, moving it in toward the center.

You want a skinny triangle. When the triangle is the size you want, press Enter (Windows) or Return (Macintosh) to set the size. Once you change the size of the triangle, it may move off the center of your guides. Use the arrow keys to nudge the triangle back to the center of the guide. The bottom vertex of the triangle should be on the vertical guide.

TIP *To scale the triangle from the center so you don't have to move it, choose Modify > Transform > Numeric Transform. Choose Scale from the pop-up menu. Deselect Constrain Proportions and then enter a smaller value for the width percentage. When you click OK, the triangle width is resized from the center.*

59

MAKING A COPY

In this next step, you need to make a copy of the triangle and move it straight down to the bottom part of the circle. You could make a copy of the triangle and then paste it on the canvas and then move the new copy to the proper place. There is an easier way, however, that makes the copy and moves it in one step.

1) Select the triangle with the Pointer tool if it is not already selected.

You see the blue handles around the selected triangle.

2) Hold down Alt (Windows) or Option (Macintosh) and drag straight down.

As you drag, the pointer adds a plus sign, indicating that you are making a copy. You actually are performing two operations: you are making a copy, and you are moving the copy a set distance from the original. Add the Shift key as you drag to vertically constrain the movement. Release the mouse button when you are at the bottom of the circle of the candy.

TIP *Release the mouse button before releasing the modifier keys (Shift, Alt, or Option) to make sure the triangle remains in place.*

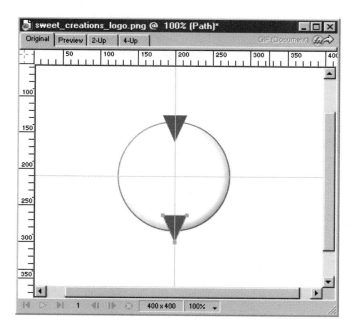

ROTATING AN OBJECT

The next step is to rotate the bottom triangle so that it points upward. You can use the Scale tool to rotate the triangle, or you can use a command. In this example, either way works fine. You might want to try both methods to see which one you prefer.

1) Select the triangle.

The triangle appears with blue handles.

2) Do one of the following:

- Choose Modify > Transform > Rotate 180°.

or

- Select the Scale tool on the Tools panel. Move the pointer close to, but not touching, the triangle. When you see the circular cursor, drag the triangle around 180 degrees.

Hold down Shift as you drag to pop to 90-degree increments as you rotate the object.

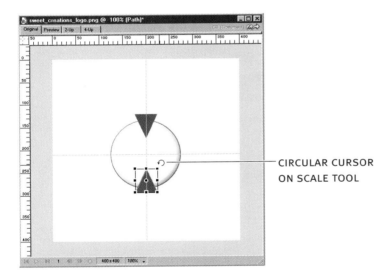

CIRCULAR CURSOR
ON SCALE TOOL

3) Press Enter (Windows) or Return (Macintosh) when you complete the rotation.

You want this second triangle the same distance within the circle as the first one. Use the arrow keys to move it up or down, if needed.

USING THE HISTORY PANEL

The History panel records each step you perform as you create objects on the canvas. Each time you choose Edit > Undo, you are stepping back a step on the History panel. The History panel makes it easy to see your steps and undo multiple actions. You can also use the History panel to repeat a set of actions. In this next exercise, you will make a copy of the triangles and then rotate them around the circle. Then you'll use the History panel to repeat the steps to add the remaining triangles to complete the drawing.

1) Select both triangles with the Pointer tool.

Select one triangle; then hold down Shift and select the other.

2) Choose Edit > Clone.

Cloning makes a copy of the object or objects and places the copy directly on top of the original object. This is the same as performing a copy operation and a paste operation in one step.

3) Choose Modify > Transform > Numeric Transform. In the Numeric Transform dialog box that appears, choose Rotate from the pop-up menu.

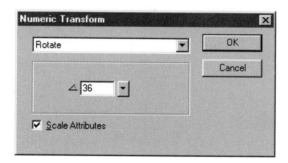

The Numeric Transform command rotates the object around its centerpoint. In this case, since you have two triangles, the centerpoint of the triangles is the centerpoint of the circle.

4) Type *36* in the Rotate text box and then click OK.

A positive number rotates the object clockwise; a negative number rotates the object counterclockwise. You now have two more triangles around the circle.

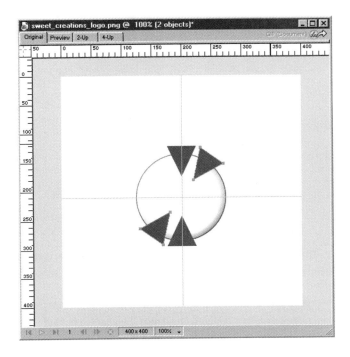

NOTE *Since there are 360 degrees in a circle, entering 36 for the rotation amount results in 10 triangles around the circle when you complete the remaining steps.*

5) Choose Window > History to open the History panel.

The History panel displays a list of all of your past actions. The number of actions saved is based on your preferences. The default number is 20. You can change this number by choosing Edit > Preferences. On the General tab, type a new number in the Undo Steps text box. You can enter any number between 0 and 100; however, a large number increases the RAM requirements for the application. Unless you have an enormous amount of free RAM, leave the default set to 20. That should be plenty for most of your work. If you do make a change to Undo Steps, you'll need to quit and then relaunch Fireworks to make the change take effect.

6) Scroll to the bottom of the History list until you see the last two actions: Clone and Transform. Hold down Shift and select the last two actions.

These last two steps need to be repeated to get more triangles around the circle.

7) Click Replay, located at the bottom left of the History panel. Two more triangles are added. Continue to click Replay until you have all the triangles around the circle.

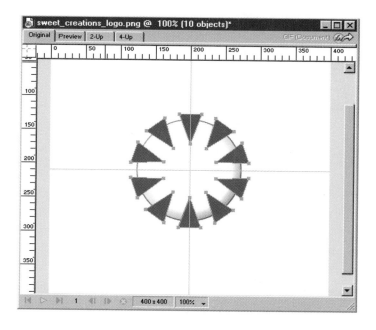

The History panel can replay steps, as you've just seen, and it can be used to step back through your actions, like a super undo function. To undo your steps with the History panel, just drag the slider on the left up; to redo the steps, drag the slider down. You can also save your steps for actions you will be performing again.

64

For example, in the preceding step, you cloned and rotated the triangles. You used the Replay button to create other triangles. If you know that you will want to perform that same action again, you can save the steps as a command.

8) Hold down Shift and select the Clone and Transform actions on the History panel if they are not already selected. You can either click the diskette icon at the bottom of the History panel or choose the Save as Command from the the Options pop-up menu on the panel. In the Save Command dialog box, type *Clone and Rotate*, and then click OK.

Those actions are now saved as a single command on the Commands menu for you to use again.

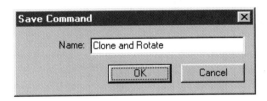

NOTE *To see how the saved command works, draw another triangle off to the side of the candy you are drawing. Choose Commands > Clone and Rotate (the command name you entered appears on the Commands menu). The triangle is cloned and then rotated. Repeat the command several more times. You don't need those extra triangles, so you can delete them for this exercise.*

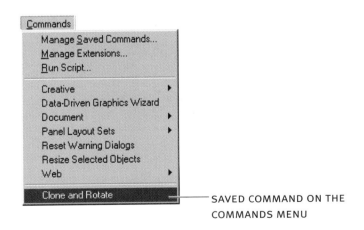

SAVED COMMAND ON THE COMMANDS MENU

MASKING WITH PASTE INSIDE

The triangles around the circle extend outside the circle. You want them contained within the circle. The problem is that the circle is curved around the edges, and the edges of the triangles are straight. To fit the triangles within the curve, you'll use a masking method called Paste Inside. Think of the circle as if it were a cookie cutter and you could use it to cut through the triangles. Then the cut edges would be curved, and the triangles would fit precisely within the circle. There are other ways to create a mask that you will learn in later lessons.

1) Select all the triangles.

You can Shift-click each triangle to select it; or an easier way is to choose Select > Select All. Select All will also select the circle, which you don't want selected. Hold down Shift and click in the middle of the circle to deselect it.

NOTE *When you hold down Shift and click an object, you alternately select or deselect the object.*

TIP *The document title bar displays the number of selected objects; 10 in this example.*

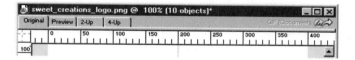

2) Choose Edit > Cut, select the circle, and then choose Edit > Paste Inside.

The triangles are pasted within the circle. Because you applied the Inner Bevel effect to the circle, the triangles take on that beveled look as well.

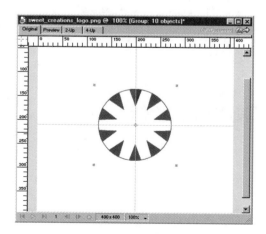

ON YOUR OWN

To add more interest to the candy, you can add other geometric designs to the center. For example, draw a small ellipse in the center of the candy. Make the ellipse the same color red as the triangles. Use the concepts you just learned to clone and then rotate the ellipse 45 degrees. Then use the History panel to repeat the steps.

GROUPING OBJECTS

Multiple objects are sometimes easier to work with if you tie them together as a unit. This is called grouping. When objects are grouped, they move together and can be manipulated as a single unit. Scaling and rotation control all objects in the group at the same time. You can also combine two groups or combine a group and an object. This is referred to as nested grouping.

1) Select the Pointer tool on the Tools panel and move the pointer over one of the ellipses in the center of the candy.

When you move over an object, red handles appear around the object. You might find this option distracting at first, but it does make it easy to determine what object you are pointing to before you actually select the object. Since the ellipse is red and the handles are red, it might be difficult to see them, but you'll see some movement when you move over one of the objects.

TIP *If you decide you don't want to see the red handles when you move over an object, you can turn off that option in the Preferences dialog box. Choose Edit > Preferences or Fireworks > Preferences (Macintosh OS X) and select Editing from the tabs (Windows) or the pop-up menu (Macintosh). Deselect Mouse Highlight from the Pointer Tool Options section of the dialog box.*

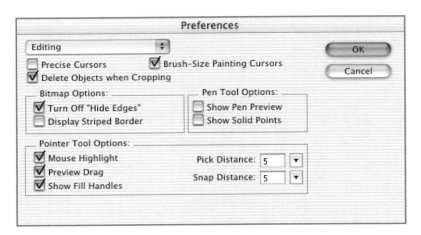

2) Hold down Shift and click each of the ellipses to select them.

You could also use the select all method as you did before and then Shift-click the candy to deselect it from the group.

3) Choose Modify > Group.

The grouped object has four blue handles around it. If you move the group to a new location, the group now moves as one.

To ungroup the objects, you would choose Modify > Ungroup.

TIP *In Windows, you can use the Group and Ungroup buttons on the Modify toolbar. Choose Window > Toolbars > Modify to access the Modify toolbar.*

4) Select both the candy and the center group and group them.

With all the elements of the logo grouped, moving the candy and the center design is easy.

IMPORTING GRAPHICS

Macromedia Fireworks provides a wealth of tools for creating graphics, but you still may want to import graphics from other sources. For example, you may want to import a company logo created in Macromedia FreeHand or import a scanned image from Adobe Photoshop to combine with buttons you've created in Fireworks.

Fireworks can import these formats: PNG; GIF; JPEG; PICT; BMP; TIFF; xRes LRG; ASCII text; RTF text; Adobe Photoshop 3, 4, 5, and 6; Adobe Illustrator 7; Macromedia FreeHand 7, 8, 9, and 10; and uncompressed CorelDRAW 7.

To finish the company logo, you need to add some text. The text was created in Macromedia FreeHand and converted to a graphic for you to use. Of course, you can add text in Fireworks, but in this case the text was created with a typeface that may not be available to you. You'll see how to convert text to a graphic in Fireworks in a later lesson.

1) Choose File > Import and navigate to the sweet_creations.fh10 file located in the Media folder within the Lesson02 folder. Select that file and then click Open.

In the Vector File Options dialog box, you can define specific settings.

Options you can set in the Vector File Options dialog box are as follows:

Scale: Specify the scale percentage for the imported file.

Width and Height: Specify in pixels the width and height of the imported file.

Resolution: Specify the resolution of the imported file.

Anti-Alias: Set a soft edge around imported objects.

File Conversion: Specify how multipage documents are handled when imported.

> **Open a Page**: Import only the specified page.
>
> **Open Pages as Frames**: Import all the pages from the document and place each on a separate frame in Fireworks.
>
> **Remember Layers**: Maintain the layer structure of the imported file.
>
> **Ignore Layers**: Delete the layer structure of the imported file. All objects are placed on the currently selected layer.
>
> **Convert Layers to Frames**: Place each layer of the imported document in a separate frame in Fireworks.
>
> **Include Invisible Layers**: Import objects on layers that have been turned off. Otherwise, invisible layers are ignored.
>
> **Include Background Layers**: Import objects from the document's Background layer. Otherwise, the Background layer is ignored.

Render as Images: Rasterize (convert to bitmap) complex groups, blends, or tiled fills and place them as a single image object in a Fireworks document. Enter a number in the text box to determine how many objects a group, blend, or tiled fill can contain before it is rasterized during import.

NOTE *Vector file options do not apply when you paste or drag an object from another application.*

2) Click OK to select the default vector options.

You don't need to make any changes for this project.

3) Click to place the text graphic on the page. Move the text to the right side of the candy and scale (hold down Shift and drag a corner handle) to make the text smaller.

You want the text to be proportional to the size of the candy. You may need to move the candy to the left of the canvas to place the text on the right. Because you grouped all the elements of the candy, they will move as one.

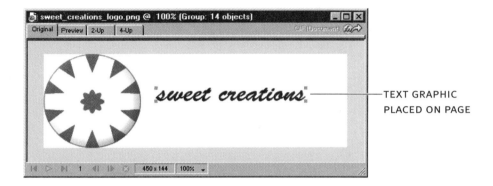

TEXT GRAPHIC
PLACED ON PAGE

4) Select both the candy and the text and then choose Modify › Group.

You now have a nested group. The candy is grouped, and that group is included with this new group.

5) Save your file.

71

TRIMMING THE CANVAS

The final step is to make the document size smaller. You need to trim the excess white area of the canvas around the image to make the image size as small as possible. You could use the Crop tool, but the easiest method is to use the built-in trimming feature.

1) Choose Modify > Canvas > Trim Canvas, and the work is done for you.

Fireworks makes the canvas as small as it can without cutting off any object. Fireworks knows the exact size and placement of all objects on the page, even if they are not visible. Soft edges such as drop shadows and glows are even accounted for and preserved on the canvas.

2) Save your file.

You'll use this logo in later exercises. For now, you can close this file.

WHAT YOU HAVE LEARNED

In this lesson, you have:

- Displayed rulers and guides to aid you in aligning objects on the page [pages 46–48]

- Added a bevel edge to a circle [pages 49–53]

- Saved a style for use on other objects [pages 55–56]

- Used the Polygon tool to draw triangles [pages 56–58]

- Used the Scale tool to change the size and rotate an object [pages 58–61]

- Repeated steps in the History panel and saved the steps as a command [pages 62–65]

- Applied masking using Paste Inside [page 66]

- Grouped items together [pages 67–68]

- Imported a graphic from FreeHand [pages 69–71]

- Trimmed the canvas [page 72]

working with layers

LESSON 3

Layers are a powerful feature that helps you manage and organize objects on your page. Layers are transparent planes where you can create and store objects. With layers, you can control the stacking order of objects on your page, quickly moving objects up or down if the stacking order changes. You can also lock and hide layers to make complex objects easier to manage.

In this lesson, you will create a Web page and use layers to control the placement of objects on the page.

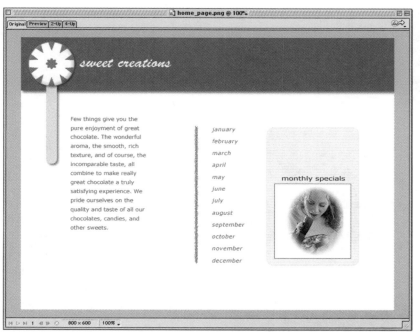

In this lesson, you will build a home page for your site, using layers to make the production easier.

WHAT YOU WILL LEARN

In this lesson, you will:

- Examine the Layers panel

- Add and name your layers

- Use the Property inspector for precise positioning and sizing of objects

- Rename and lock a layer

- Show and hide a layer

- Use the Rounded Rectangle tool

- Add a texture and a drop shadow

- Change the stacking order of a layer

- Use single-layer editing

- Use the default fill and stroke colors

- Align objects

APPROXIMATE TIME

This lesson takes approximately 1 hour to complete.

LESSON FILES

Media Files:
Lesson03\Media\basic_colors.png

Starting Files:
Lesson03\Start\start.png

Completed Projects:
Lesson03\Completed\home_page.png

USING THE LAYERS PANEL

You can think of a layer as a transparent plane where you can create and place objects. Layers enable you to divide your artwork when building complex or composite images. Different portions of the image can be stored on different layers and selectively turned off or on so you can isolate just the portion you are working on. Layers can contain either vector or bitmap objects, or a combination of both.

The Layers panel in Fireworks is similar to layers panels in other graphics programs such as Macromedia FreeHand and Adobe Photoshop, but it includes additional information.

On each layer, you can place one object or multiple objects. If you place multiple objects on the same layer, each object is placed on the layer as an individual object within a stack of objects. New objects are initially placed on top of the stack. A thumbnail representation of the object is displayed to the left of the object name on the Layers panel. You can control the stacking order of each object in the stack using Modify > Arrange > Bring to Front, Modify > Arrange > Bring Forward, Modify > Arrange > Send to Back, and Modify > Arrange > Send Backward, or you can use the Layers panel to drag the object to a new position within the stack or move the object to a new layer.

Layers let you organize your drawings into distinct levels that can be edited as individual units or hidden from view when needed. The following exercise demonstrates how to use the Layers panel to add new layers, move objects between layers, and hide and lock layers.

1) Begin by creating a new document. Set the canvas size to 800 pixels for the width and 600 pixels for the height and make the canvas color white.

This document will become the home page for the Web site pages you are creating in these lessons.

In the early days of the Web, most users had 13-inch monitors. The price of monitors has dropped greatly, and now more users have 17-inch monitors. Today, most Web designers build their pages based on the larger 17-inch size: 800 x 600 pixels. When designing your Web pages, you need to determine the smallest screen size of your users and design the pages accordingly.

2) Save the document as *home_page.png* in the Lesson03 folder.

The name you give your Fireworks document is used for the exported HTML page. When naming your documents, you need to keep this in mind and follow some basic rules:

- Use lowercase names for your files. Some Web servers are case sensitive; some require that you use only lowercase file names.

- Don't use spaces within your file names. Use the underscore or dash character to simulate a space to separate words. For example, use home_page.htm instead of home page.htm.

- Use letters and numbers, but no special characters such as %, *, or /.

3) Choose Window > Layers.

If the Layers panel was closed, it is opened. A check next to the panel name in the menu list indicates that the panel is open. If you see the panel in the panel group on the right of your screen, you can also click the expander arrow on the panel to open or close it. For this exercise, you might want to close any other panels so you see only the Layers panel.

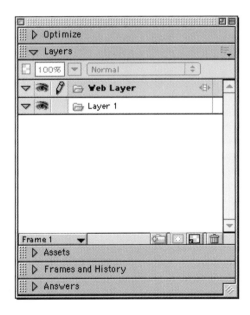

4) Move the pointer to the title bar of the panel just below the Layers panel.

When you are over the title bar of a panel below an open panel, the pointer changes to an up-and-down-pointing arrow in Windows and a down-pointing arrow on the Macintosh. When you see the pointer change, you can drag down to increase or decrease the height of the panel above. Once you begin adding layers, you'll want to increase the size of the Layers panel.

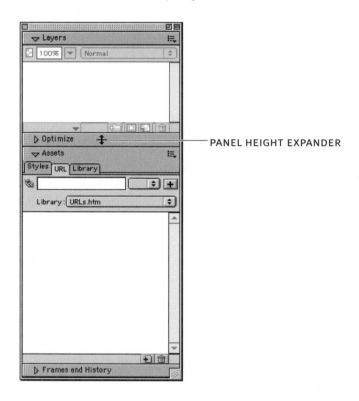

PANEL HEIGHT EXPANDER

NOTE *You can only increase or decrease a panel if two panels are open.*

ADDING AND NAMING LAYERS

When you create a new document, you get two layers by default: Layer 1 and the Web Layer. The Web Layer is where slices and hotspots are stored. We'll discuss these in a later lesson.

Layer 1 is where all your objects and images are placed initially. If you don't create any other layer, all the objects in your document will be stacked in this layer. For single drawings—the logo you created in Lesson 2 for example—having all objects on the same layer works just fine.

For more complex pages, using layers is a good way to organize and manage the different elements you create. You can lock any layer, allowing you to work on one part of the page without accidentally moving or deleting an object, or you can hide a layer so you won't be distracted by its elements as you create another portion of the page.

1) Click the Layers panel Options menu, located at the top right of the panel title bar, and choose New Layer from the pop-up menu.

The panel Options menu contains several commands for modifying or controlling layers. All panels (not just the Layers panel) display the Options menu icon when the panel is open.

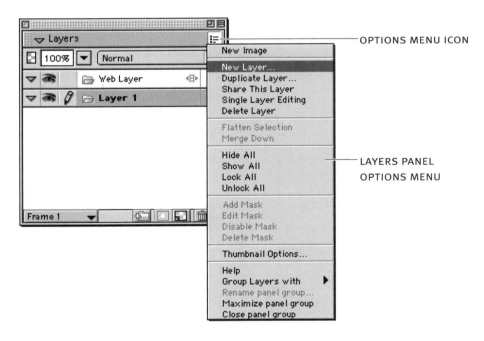

79

2) Type *Logo* in the New Layer dialog box and click OK.

A new layer named Logo is added above the Layer 1 layer.

The new layer is selected. Look on the Layers panel, and you'll see a pencil icon. This icon indicates the selected layer. Anything you add to the document is placed on the selected layer.

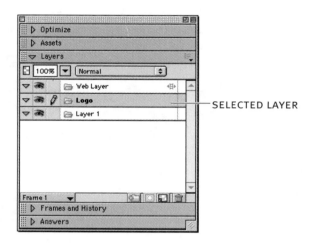

SELECTED LAYER

◎ POWER TIP *You can also click the New Layer icon at the bottom of the Layers panel. This creates a new layer with the default name Layer 1, Layer 2, and so on. If you add a layer using this method, you do not get the dialog box for naming the layer. See the section "Renaming a Layer" later in this lesson to learn how to change the default layer names.*

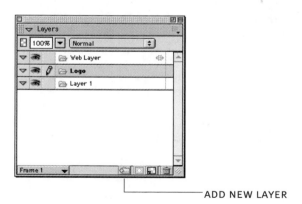

ADD NEW LAYER

3) Choose File › Import and locate the sweet_creations_logo.png file you created in Lesson 2 and click Open.

If you can't find the file, you can use the file in the Completed folder in Lesson 2.

4) Click when you see the right-angle pointer.

The place you click is where the logo is placed on the canvas. You want the logo at the top left of the canvas.

The logo is placed on the Logo layer.

5) Click Layer 1 on the Layers panel to select that layer.

This is the default layer. Because it is below the Logo layer, anything you place on this layer will be underneath the logo on the canvas.

6) Select the Rectangle tool from the Tools panel and then draw a rectangle at the top of the page. Make the rectangle as wide as the page.

Notice that the rectangle is underneath the logo. Don't worry about the color of the rectangle; you'll change it later.

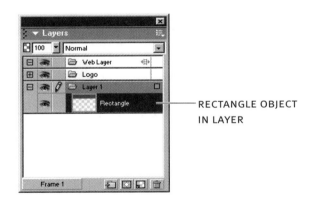

RECTANGLE OBJECT
IN LAYER

ADJUSTING THE SIZE AND PLACEMENT OF AN OBJECT

Often you'll want to control or check the size of an object you've drawn. In this exercise, you have a rectangle on the page. You might have placed it exactly at the top of the page, but you want to verify that it is exact. You also want to verify that it is the same size as the canvas—800 pixels in this example.

With the rectangle selected, look at the Property inspector. The left section of the panel displays information about the rectangle: its size and placement on the canvas.

1) In the Property inspector, enter _800_ for the width of the rectangle and _118_ for the height of the rectangle.

NOTE *The height of the rectangle should be larger than the height of the candy logo. If your logo is larger, you may need to adjust the rectangle height.*

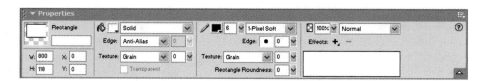

2) Enter _0_ (zero) for both the X and Y values of the rectangle in the Property inspector.

This places the rectangle at the top left of the canvas.

TIP *You can press the Tab key to move to the next text box in the Property inspector. To set the values, press Enter (Windows) or Return (Macintosh) or click outside the panel.*

RENAMING A LAYER

The layer name for the rectangle is Layer 1. As you add more layers to your document, it is helpful to give each layer a descriptive name.

1) Double-click the name in the panel.

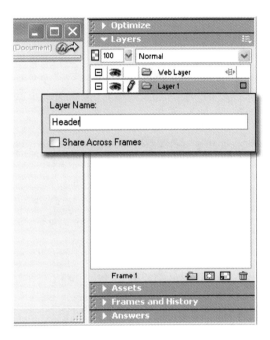

2) In the Layer Name pop-up window, type *Header* and then press Enter (Windows) or Return (Macintosh).

LOCKING A LAYER

Locking a layer is helpful when you want to see all of the objects on the layer, but you don't want to accidentally move or delete any objects. Locking a layer also prevents you from adding new objects to that layer.

1) Select the logo.

Notice when you select the logo that the selected layer on the Layers panel changes to the Logo layer.

2) Resize and move the logo to make it fit within the height of the rectangle.

You can use the Scale tool as you learned in Lesson 2, or you can use the Pointer tool to drag one of the corner handles to change the size. Because all of the elements in the logo are grouped, all elements will be scaled together.

◎ POWER TIP *If you use the Scale tool, you just need to drag one of the corner handles to resize the logo. If you use the Pointer tool, then you also need to hold down Shift as you drag a corner handle to proportionally scale the logo.*

3) Click the Lock column (the column that displays a pencil) to the left of the Logo layer to lock the layer so its objects can't be moved or deleted.

A lock icon appears in the column.

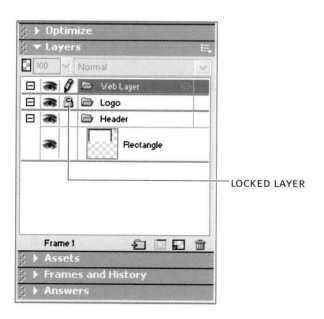

LOCKED LAYER

If a layer is currently selected, the Lock column displays a pencil. When you click the pencil, the Lock column displays a lock. A blank Lock column means the layer is not selected.

When the layer is locked, you cannot select the layer or the objects on the layer. To unlock the layer, click the lock icon on the Layers panel.

⊙ **P O W E R   T I P** *Hold down Alt (Windows) or Option (Macintosh) and click the Lock column to lock or unlock all layers at once.*

SHOWING AND HIDING A LAYER

If you have a complex drawing, it is sometimes helpful to display only the portions of the drawing that you are currently working on. This way, you don't accidentally delete or move another object that might be overlapping the object that you are modifying.

1) Select the Header layer and click the Show/Hide column (the eye icon).

The rectangle is hidden.

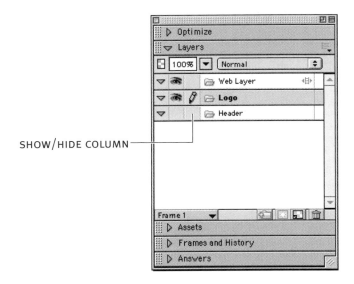

SHOW/HIDE COLUMN

2) Click the Show/Hide column again to display the objects on the layer.

⊙ **P O W E R   T I P** *Hold down Alt (Windows) or Option (Macintosh) as you click any Show/Hide icon to make all layers visible.*

PICKING COLORS

The colors you use on your Web pages can be from a set palette of colors, or you can choose from an unlimited number of colors. Perhaps you want to limit the colors you use to match a product line or company colors. To make it easier to pick only those colors, you can create a document containing those colors.

1) Open the basic_colors.png file in the Lesson03 folder.

The document opens on top of your existing document. It contains a set of boxes, each with a different color.

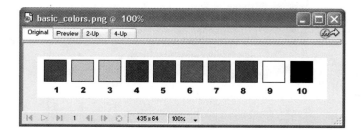

2) Choose Window > Tile Vertical.

Both windows are sized to fit side by side based on the size of your monitor. You could do this manually, but the command is much quicker.

You could also choose Tile Horizontal to resize and move one window below the other. When you want to return the windows to their original size and placement, choose Window > Cascade.

NOTE *Macintosh users: The tile commands are available only in Windows. Resize the windows and move them side by side.*

3) Select the rectangle on your home page.

You want to change the rectangles's fill color to the red color (color number 1) in the basic_colors.png file.

4) Click the Fill color box in the Property inspector and move the eyedropper over the red color in the basic_colors.png file. Click to select that color.

The color of the rectangle changes to red.

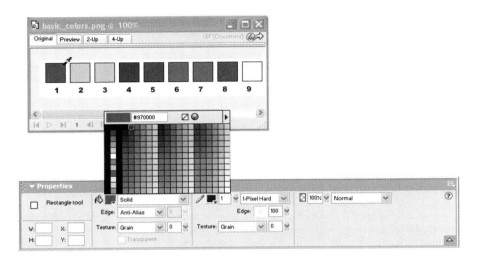

NOTE *You could also use the Fill color box on the Tools panel to change the color. The color boxes are located in several places: the Property inspector, the Tools panel, and the Colors panel.*

5) Unlock the Logo layer.

Click the lock icon on the Logo layer to unlock the layer.

6) Select the logo and choose Modify > Ungroup. Click outside the logo to deselect it and then select the Sweet Creations text. Change the fill color of the text to white.

Leave the Logo layer unlocked.

USING THE ROUNDED RECTANGLE TOOL

The Rounded Rectangle tool draws rectangles with rounded edges. You can change the corner roundness amount in the Property inspector. You can also use the Rectangle tool and change the corner roundness to achieve the same effect. In these steps, you will add another element to the logo; a stick (like an ice cream stick) for the candy.

1) Select the Rounded Rectangle tool and draw a vertical rectangle on the left side of the page.

The rectangle has a fill of white. Fireworks remembers the last color you applied to an object. In the last steps, you changed the color of the text to white.

⊙ POWER TIP *After you draw the rectangle, you can always move it to a new location. You also have the option of moving the object as you draw. Hold down the Spacebar as you drag. Now you can move the rectangle to a new location before you release the mouse button. When you release the Spacebar, the rectangle locks in place, and you can continue to resize it. You can use the Spacebar move operation with any of the rectangle or ellipse tools or the bitmap marquee tools.*

2) Change the color of the rectangle to color number 2 (a light tan) in the basic_colors.png file.

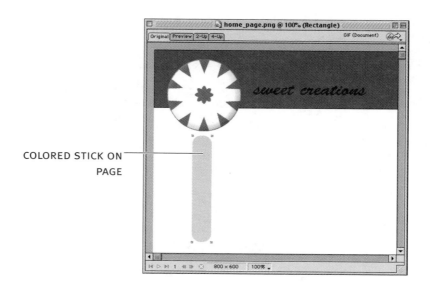

COLORED STICK ON
PAGE

3) If you have the basic_colors.png file placed to the right of your home page file, choose Window > Cascade (Windows only) to return the windows to their original size and placement.

If you have a large monitor, you can leave the two windows side by side.

4) Drag the Rectangle Roundness slider in the Property inspector to 90.

You could also type the value you want in the text box. Press Enter (Windows) or Return (Macintosh) to enter the value for the rectangle.

5) Select the Pointer tool and drag the stick over the candy in the logo. Resize the rectangle to make it proportional to the candy.

You can change the size of the stick by dragging one of the handles with the Pointer tool.

ADDING TEXTURE AND A DROP SHADOW

To make the stick more realistic, you will add a wood texture. Textures are grayscale images that simulate a surface blended with the fill of the object. Adding a texture changes the intensity of the fill of an object. A texture of zero percent has no effect on the image. Increasing the texture value intensifies the effect on the fill. Textures can be applied to patterns, solids, gradient fills, and even strokes.

1) Select Wood from the Texture pop-up menu in the Property inspector.

As you drag through the list, a sample of the texture is displayed to the side of the list.

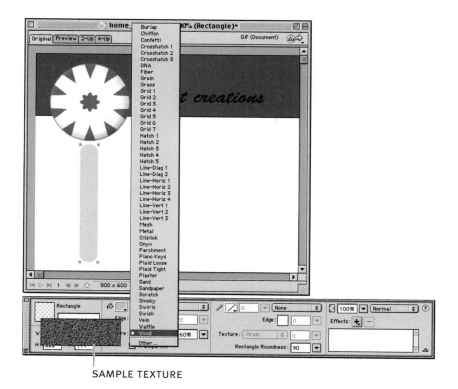

SAMPLE TEXTURE

2) Drag the amount slider to change the intensity of the texture.

For this example, try 50 percent.

TIP *Every fill has a texture applied to it. When the texture amount is set to zero percent, the texture is not visible.*

3) Add a drop shadow to the stick.

In Lesson 2, you added a bevel to the candy. You add a drop shadow in the same way. Click the Add Effects button in the Property inspector. Choose Shadow and Glow > Drop Shadow from the list. Adjust the settings to your liking.

CHANGING THE STACKING ORDER ON A LAYER

The order in which objects appear on a stack depends on the order in which they were created. Just as in other graphics programs, the last object created is on top. You can also change the stacking order of individual objects by using the Arrange submenu (on the Modify menu). The stacking order on a layer is different from the order of the layers. An object can be at the top of the object list and still be underneath an object on a higher layer. Choose Modify > Arrange > Bring to Front to bring the object to the front, or choose Modify > Arrange > Send to Back to move the object to the back. Choose Modify > Arrange > Bring Forward to bring the object in front of another object on the same layer, or choose Modify > Arrange > Send Backward to move the object behind another object on the same layer. In Windows only, you can also use the Modify toolbar for these menu options.

On the Layers panel, you now have three objects on the Logo layer: the candy, the Sweet Creations text, and the stick. Each object appears in its own stack on the layer. The stick was the last element you created, so it is on top. You want the stick beneath the candy.

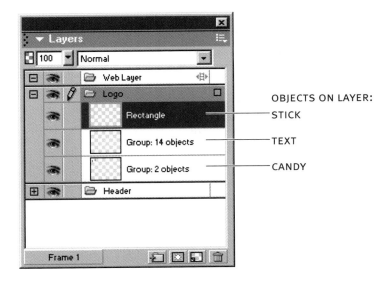

1) Select the stick.

This is the object you want to move.

2) Do one of the following:

• Choose Modify > Arrange > Send to Back.

The stick moves beneath the candy, but above the red rectangle. The rectangle is on another layer (Header) that is below the Logo layer.

or

• Drag the object (labeled Rectangle on the Logo layer) below the grouped candy object on the Layers panel.

As you drag the object on the layer, you'll see a black line appear either above or below the other objects. The object you are dragging moves to the position of the black line when you release the mouse.

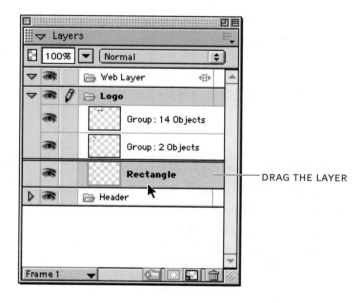

DRAG THE LAYER

Be careful as you drag not to move the rectangle object to the Header layer below. If you do, drag it back to the Logo layer.

TIP   *If you lock the other layers (Header in this example), then you can't inadvertently move an object to that layer.*

USING SINGLE-LAYER EDITING

Single-layer editing, accessed from the Layers panel Options pop-up menu, makes only the currently selected layer accessible for editing. Objects on other layers cannot be selected. This is a little different from locking the layer and can be very handy when you are working with a complex image using many layers. When you lock a layer, you can't select, edit, or change any objects on that layer until you unlock the layer. With single-layer editing, you can edit only objects on the selected layer; the other layers act as if they were locked. To select objects on other layers, you need to select the layer on the Layers panel.

1) Use the Layers panel Options menu to choose Single Layer Editing.

A check mark (Windows) or a bullet (Macintosh) appears next to the command to indicate that it is selected. This option is a toggle. To deselect the option, choose the command again from the Layers panel Options pop-up menu.

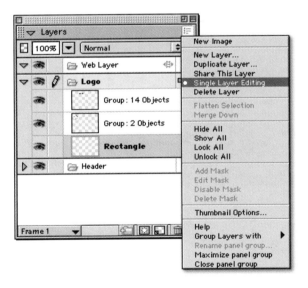

2) Make sure nothing is selected on the canvas and then select the Header layer on the Layers panel.

Choose Select > Deselect or click outside the canvas area (but still within the document window) to deselect all objects on the page. Try to select the candy or the Sweet Creations text. With the Header layer selected on the Layers panel, you can't select any object on another layer.

3) Select the Logo layer on the Layers panel.

Now try to select the rectangle on the Header layer. Again, it is not on the selected layer and so cannot be selected.

4) Turn off single-layer editing.

TIP *While single-layer editing can be very helpful, it can also be frustrating if you don't realize it is on. If you are having difficulties selecting items on the canvas, check that the layer is not locked and that Single Layer Editing is not selected.*

5) Save your file.

ON YOUR OWN

Create a new layer and name it Specials. Draw a vertical rectangle with rounded corners on the Specials layer. Make the rectangle 199 pixels wide and 305 pixels tall and the rectangle roundness 16. Move the rectangle to the right of the page. Make the fill color of the rectangle a light gray or choose color 3 from the basic_colors.png file. Add the Piano Keys texture and set the texture amount to 50 percent.

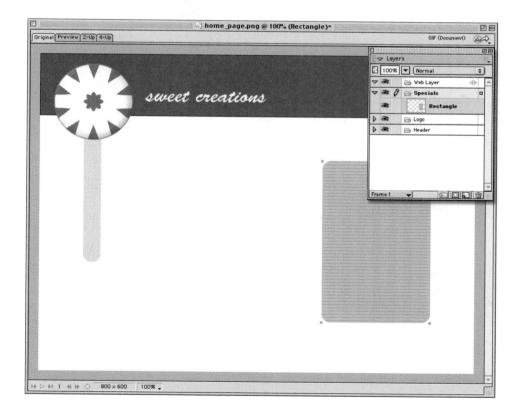

SETTING THE DEFAULT COLORS

Perhaps by now you have discovered that Fireworks retains the stroke and fill of the
last object you created and uses those settings until you change them. This is a great
feature, especially when you are adding multiple objects. Fireworks also has a set
of default fill and stroke colors. The default fill color is white, and the default stroke
color is black. You can easily change these colors to suit your needs. To change the
default colors, choose Edit > Preferences. On the General tab of the Preferences
dialog box, click the Stroke or Fill color box and pick a new default color.

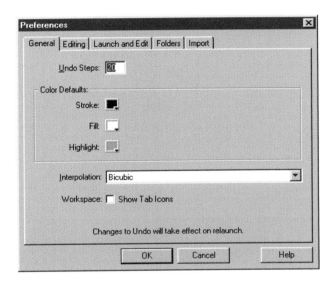

The last thing you created was the rectangle with the gray fill and the Piano Keys
texture. If you draw another rectangle, it will have the same stroke and fill. In the
next exercise, you will draw a square, but it needs to be filled with white. You could
draw the square and then change the fill color, but to save a step, you will apply the
default colors before you draw the new object.

1) Click the Default Colors button on the Tools panel.

The Fill color box changes to white (or the fill color you defined if you changed your preferences), and the Stroke color box changes to black (or the stroke color you defined if you changed your preferences).

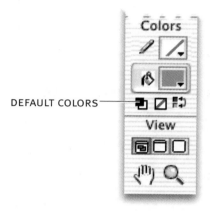

DEFAULT COLORS

2) Click the Swap Default Colors button on the Tools panel.

The fill and stroke colors are reversed. For the next exercise, you want a fill of white and a stroke of black, so click the Swap Default Colors button again.

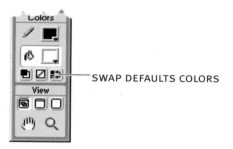

SWAP DEFAULTS COLORS

◉ POWER TIP *Press D to apply the default colors to a selected object; press X to swap the stroke and fill colors of a selected object.*

ALIGNING OBJECTS

When you are creating several objects on your page, you may want to align the objects with each other or align them to the canvas. You can also distribute objects equally on the page.

1) Draw a square on the Specials layer. Use the Rectangle tool and hold down Shift as you draw to constrain the rectangle to a square.

The square needs to be white (no texture) with a stroke of black. If you did not set your colors to the default colors in the last exercise, use the Power Tip and press D to apply the defaults to the square.

2) Use the Property inspector to change the size of the square to 165 pixels.

Make sure you change both the width and the height of the rectangle to 165 pixels to ensure that you have a square.

3) Move the square on top of the other rectangle you created in the "On Your Own" section. Place it toward the bottom of the other rectangle. Then select both rectangles.

You can Shift-click each rectangle to select the rectangles, or you can use the selection rectangle to select them. When you click and drag on the canvas, a selection rectangle appears. All objects within the selection rectangle are selected when you release the mouse button.

4) Choose Modify > Align > Center Vertical.

The square and rectangle are centered along the vertical axis.

Fireworks aligns objects on the left based on the leftmost object in the selected group, and it aligns objects on the right based on the rightmost object in the selected group. The topmost object controls Align Top, and the bottommost object controls Align Bottom. For Distribute Widths, Fireworks creates an equal amount of space between the objects, divided between the right edge of the leftmost and left edge of the rightmost objects. For Distribute Heights, Fireworks creates an equal amount of space between the objects, divided between the bottom edge of the highest and top edge of the lowest objects.

NOTE *In Windows, you can also use the alignment buttons located on the Modify toolbar. If this toolbar is not visible, choose Window > Toolbars > Modify. This toolbar can float on the screen as an independent window, or you can manually attach it to the top or bottom of the application window by dropping it there.*

You can also use the Align panel to align objects. Choose Window > Align to open the panel. The Align panel contains all the alignment options found on the Modify menu as well as an option to align objects to the canvas, an option to create equal spacing between objects, and an option to match widths or heights of objects.

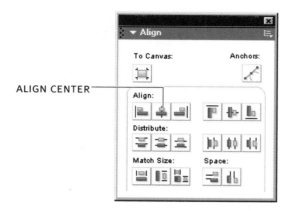

ALIGN CENTER

NOTE *The Align panel is a third-party extension added to your Fireworks application. To find more extensions, choose Commands > Manage Extensions. The Macromedia Extension Manager window opens. Then choose File > Go to Macromedia Exchange. Your Web browser opens and takes you to the Macromedia Web site where you can search for new extensions for Macromedia Flash, Fireworks, and Dreamweaver.*

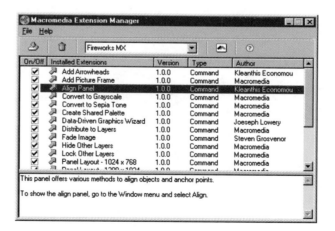

5) Choose File > Import and locate the start.png file you created in Lesson 1.

This is the image of the girl with the candy within an oval with a feathered edge. You can use the file in the Start folder in Lesson03 if you can't locate the file you created.

6) Make sure the Specials layer is still selected before you place the image; then place the image on the white square.

If you need to size the image to fit within the square, you can use the Scale tool to make it smaller or hold down Shift as you drag a corner.

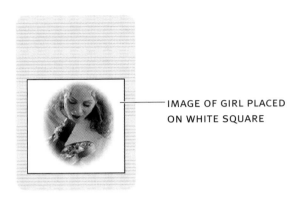

IMAGE OF GIRL PLACED
ON WHITE SQUARE

NOTE *You can scale a bitmap image smaller, but don't make it larger. The resolution of this image is 72 pixels—the standard for a Web image. The lower resolution of the image does not contain enough pixel information to allow you to increase the size of the image. Making the image larger reduces the image quality.*

7) Save your file.

You can leave this file open for the next lesson.

WHAT YOU HAVE LEARNED

In this lesson, you have:

- Created new layers and moved objects to those layers [pages 76–81]
- Used the Property inspector to move and resize an object on the canvas [page 82]
- Renamed a layer [page 83]
- Locked a layer to preserve its contents [page 84]
- Used the Rounded Rectangle tool [pages 88–89]
- Added a texture and a drop shadow to an object [pages 90–91]
- Moved objects in a layer to change the stacking order of objects [pages 91–92]
- Used single-layer editing [pages 93–94]
- Set the default colors [pages 95–96]
- Aligned objects on the canvas [pages 97–98].

adding text

Fireworks MX is a very powerful graphics program for creating Web and interactive images. No matter how creative and informative your images are, though, you will still want to provide labels for your buttons and text for your banner ads. Fireworks provides many features for applying and formatting text in your images.

Text in a Fireworks document saved in the original PNG file format is always editable. However, after you export the image as a GIF or JPEG file, the text becomes part of the bitmap image and cannot be changed. Thus, you should always keep the original Fireworks file (the PNG file) along with the exported images in case the text needs to be changed. In this lesson, you will add text to the Web page you began creating in Lesson 3.

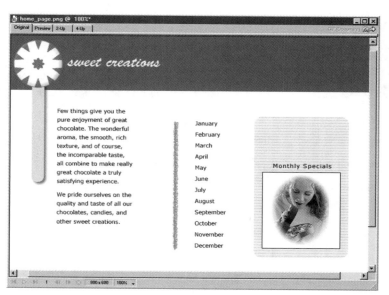

In this lesson, you will add text to the home page and learn the text formatting controls.

WHAT YOU WILL LEARN

In this lesson, you will:

- Add and format text

- Use the spell checker

- Use the Text Editor

- Use the Line and Subselection tools

- Use the Paste Attributes command

APPROXIMATE TIME

This lesson takes approximately 1 hour to complete.

LESSON FILES

Media Files:
Lesson04\Media\intro.txt

Starting Files:
Lesson04\Start\home_page_L4.png

Completed Projects:
Lesson04\Completed\home_page_L4.png

ADDING TEXT

You add text to a document by using the Text tool. This tool is similar to text tools in other graphics programs. When you select the tool, the Property inspector displays all the text formatting controls. You can make formatting changes before you even type your text or change the text once it is on the page.

1) Open the home_page.png file you created in Lesson 3.

If you no longer have the file, you can use the file home_page_L4.png in the Start folder within the Lesson04 folder. Choose File > Save As and leave off the L4 in the file name and save this new file in the Lesson04 folder.

2) Select the Specials layer on the Layers panel.

The text you are adding will be placed on the Specials layer.

3) Choose the Text tool on the Tools panel.

The pointer changes to the I-beam pointer, indicating that you are in text editing mode.

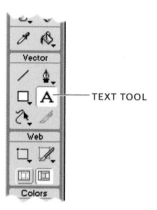

TEXT TOOL

4) Click where you want the text to start, or click and drag to draw a text box of the desired size. Type _Monthly Specials_.

For this exercise, click (or click and drag) above the white square with the image of the girl. Make sure you are not within the white square.

Monthly Specials ————— ADD MONTHLY SPECIALS TEXT

TIP _If you click and drag with the Text tool, you can draw the text box the exact width you need. The text box indicates this with a hollow square handle at the top right of the text box. If you just click with the Text tool on the canvas, the text box expands horizontally based on the amount of text. The text box indicates this with a hollow circle handle at the top right of the text box. To switch from one type of text box to the other, double-click either the circle or square._

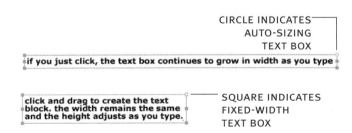

CIRCLE INDICATES
AUTO-SIZING
TEXT BOX

if you just click, the text box continues to grow in width as you type

click and drag to create the text block. the width remains the same and the height adjusts as you type.

SQUARE INDICATES
FIXED-WIDTH
TEXT BOX

⊙ POWER TIP _To resize the text box as you type, move the pointer over the bottom right handle. The cursor changes to an arrow pointer where you can drag the handle to resize the text box. Move the pointer back within the text box, and it returns to the I-beam, and you can continue to type. Changing the size of an auto-sizing text box converts it to a fixed-width text box._

5) Switch to the Pointer tool.

With the Pointer tool, you can move the text block around on the canvas, and you can make formatting changes.

TIP *If you are formatting all the text the same way, you can select the text with the Pointer tool and make your changes. If you want to selectively change the text, you need to select that text with the Text tool and then make your changes, just as you would in a word processor.*

6) Format the text using the controls in the Property inspector. Change the font to Verdana (or Arial if Verdana is not on your machine). Change the point size to *12*. Change the color of the text to black.

Use the Font pop-up list to change the font. Use the Size slider (or type a number) to change the point size. Use the Fill color box pop-up window to change the color of the selected text.

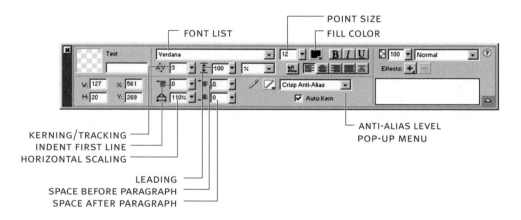

TIP *Text displays better when your view magnification is set to 100 percent.*

7) Drag the Horizontal Scale slider to change the text.

You can alter text by using a technique called horizontal scaling. This changes the width of the text without changing the height, as if you were stretching the text on a rubber band. Be careful not to overdo the stretching; you are electronically distorting the text without regard to its original design. The values are expressed as percentages. Values less than 100 percent condense the text; values greater than 100 percent expand the text.

8) Drag the Kerning slider to adjust the spacing between the letters.

Range kerning (also referred to as tracking in other programs) controls the amount of space between the selected letters. Negative values decrease the space; positive values increase the space. You can select all of the text (as you have in this exercise) or just portions of the text and then apply this formatting.

TIP *This formatting control can make smaller text sizes easier to read on the screen.*

Kerning is the amount of space between two letters. The same slider controls this formatting. If the I-beam is between two letters, you are kerning; if you have two or more letters selected, you are applying range kerning. As with range kerning, negative values decrease the space; positive values increase the space.

9) Choose the Text tool and click to the left of the gray rectangle. Type the months of the year, pressing Enter (Windows) or Return (Macintosh) after each month.

If you happen to misspell one of the months, don't correct it yet. You'll check your spelling in the next exercise.

January
February
March
April
May
June
July
August
September
October
November
December

Monthly Specials

10) Select all the text you just entered, either by dragging with the Text tool or selecting the text block with the Pointer tool. Drag the Leading slider to 200 percent.

LEADING SLIDER

When you have text with two or more lines, you may need to adjust the spacing between the lines: the leading. The term leading (pronounced "ledding") comes from the days of manual typesetting, when lead bars were placed between the rows of metal type. The size of the bar controlled the spacing between the lines of type.

Numbers less than 100 percent tighten the spacing between the lines; numbers greater than 100 percent increase the spacing between the lines.

Experiment with the leading amount and make the month text block as tall as the gray rectangle to the right.

TIP *Leading defaults to a percentage amount, but you can use a pixel amount instead. Change the selection in the Leading Units pop-up menu to Pixels and then adjust the Leading slider.*

11) If necessary, change the anti-aliasing setting to make your text easier to read.

Notice the soft edges around the text. That softness is caused by the anti-aliasing controls. Anti-aliasing is a method of blurring the edges around objects so they appear smooth on the screen. With large-sized text, the smoothness enhances the appearance of the text. On smaller text, the anti-aliasing sometimes causes the characters to blur together. You can control text anti-aliasing from the Anti-Alias level pop-up menu in the Property inspector.

Your choices here are No Anti-Alias, Crisp Anti-Alias, Strong Anti-Alias, and Smooth Anti-Alias. Experiment with each setting to determine the best choice.

ALIGNING AND INDENTING TEXT

You can change the alignment of your text relative to the text box. Click one of the alignment buttons on the Property inspector to change the alignment. To fit text within a set space, you can set the alignment to stretch the text.

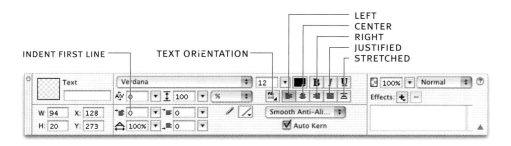

To indent the first line of a paragraph, enter the amount of indentation in pixels in the Indent First line text box. You can also change the text orientation. The default is horizontal left to right.

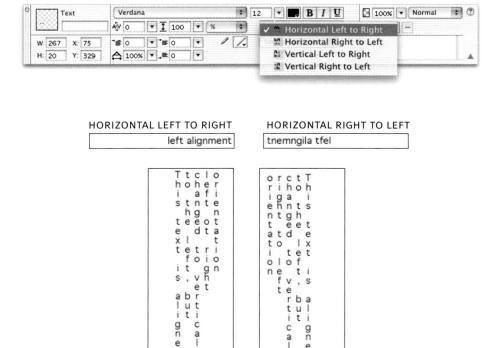

CHECKING YOUR SPELLING

There are plenty of ways to make your Web site look unprofessional, but misspelling words doesn't need to be part of the list. There is nothing unique about the spell checker in Fireworks—it works just like spell checkers in word processors or other applications you've used. When Fireworks locates a word not in its dictionary, it presents you with a list of suggested words for you to choose from, or you can save the word to your user dictionary.

1) Choose Text > Spelling Setup.

In the Spelling Setup dialog box, you can pick the dictionary to use for the spell check. There are also several options for words to ignore during the spell check.

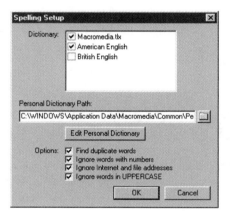

2) Choose the dictionary you want to use from the Dictionary list and select or deselect from the list of options to use during the spell check.

If you don't choose a dictionary, an alert message appears when you check spelling in your document.

3) Click Edit Personal Dictionary.

Here, you can type any special words that might be flagged during a spell check. Press Enter (Windows) or Return (Macintosh) after each word you enter.

NOTE *The spelling dictionaries are stored in a location that is common to both Fireworks MX and Dreamweaver MX. When you add a word to your personal dictionary in Fireworks MX, it is available for you to use in Dreamweaver MX.*

For example, if your company name or product name is not in the dictionary, you can add it here. The next time you perform a spell check, any word you've added to the dictionary is considered correct and so ignored.

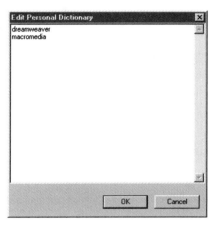

4) Click OK to exit the Personal Dictionary dialog box and then click OK to exit the Spelling Setup dialog box. Choose Text > Check Spelling and then click OK when the spelling check is complete.

If the spell checker finds a misspelled word, it flags the word and suggests an alternative. You can choose that word, pick from a list of other suggestions, or type the corrected spelling in the Change To text box. You can also choose to ignore the word or to add the word to your personal dictionary.

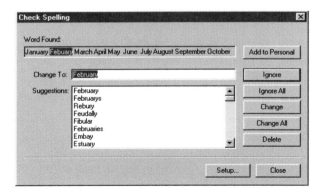

NOTE *If you have a text block selected when you choose the Check Spelling command, Fireworks checks all the words in that text box and then asks whether you want to continue checking the remainder of the document. If no text box is selected, then the entire document is checked.*

IMPORTING TEXT

You can type text directly in Fireworks, or you can import text that was created in another application and saved as RTF (Rich Text Format) or ASCII text. Remember that all text in Fireworks is converted to a graphic when you export to HTML, and text that is a graphic takes longer to download than regular text on an HTML page. Sometimes, though, you will want to use text as a graphic: as labels for buttons, as part of a logo, or to create text that looks the same no matter what fonts users have on their systems. For instance, the months-of-the-year text you just created will be converted to buttons in a later lesson.

1) Choose File > Import and locate the intro.txt file in the Media folder within the Lesson04 folder. Click Open.

Fireworks displays only valid files for you to choose from in the Import dialog box. For text files, only ASCII or RTF text files are displayed.

> **NOTE** *To save a file created in Microsoft Word as an ASCII file, choose Text Only as the Save as Type option.*

2) Click to the right of the stick in the logo.

The text block is placed on the page where you click. Move and resize the text with the Pointer tool.

3) Change the font to Verdana and the font size to 12 and increase the leading amount to 160 percent.

You may need to adjust the width of the text block as you change the formatting.

USING THE TEXT EDITOR

As you've seen in this lesson, you can type, edit, and format your text on the canvas with the Text tool. If you have small type, it is sometimes difficult to see the text on your screen. You can increase the view magnification, or you can use the Text Editor.

The Text Editor, as its name implies, is a separate window where you can type, edit, and format text on the page. You first need to add the text using the Text tool. Once the text is on the page, you can access the Text Editor.

1) With the Pointer tool, select the text block you just imported and then choose Text > Editor.

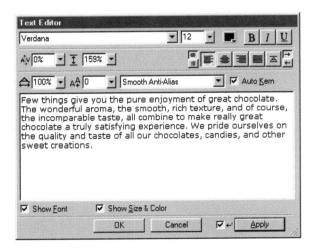

The Text Editor window contains most of the formatting controls for your text. Just as in a word processor, you need to select the text you want to change if you are making formatting changes. If you want the formatted text displayed in the Text Editor window, select Show Font and Show Size and Color. If you want the text you type constantly updated in the document window, select the Auto-Apply check box (to the left of the Apply button). If you don't select Auto-Apply, you can click Apply to update the document window.

TIP *You can position the text block on the page even while you are in the Text Editor. The pointer becomes the Hand tool when you move outside the Text Editor window.*

2) Press Enter (Windows) or Return (Macintosh) before the last sentence to create a new paragraph; then click OK.

Your new paragraph is not set apart from the other paragraph because the spacing between the paragraphs is the same as the leading (the space between the lines). In the next step, you will add extra space between the paragraphs.

3) In the Property inspector, drag the Space After Paragraph slider to 10.

This control adds space (in points) after each paragraph in the text block. Adjust the spacing to your liking. You might have noticed that you can also adjust spacing before the paragraphs. (Typically, you use one of the paragraph spacing controls, but not both.) You can also add an indent amount for each paragraph.

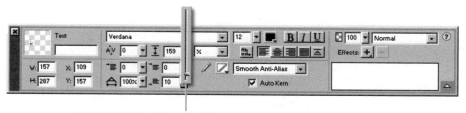

SPACE AFTER PARAGRAPH POP-UP SLIDER

NOTE *The paragraph spacing and indent controls are not available in the Text Editor.*

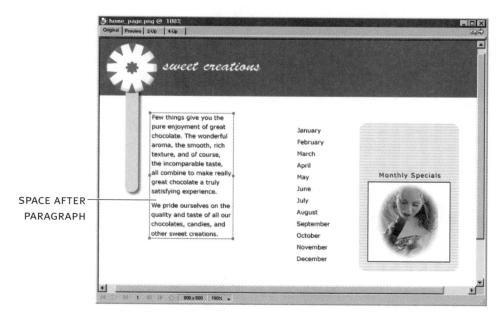

SPACE AFTER PARAGRAPH

USING THE LINE TOOL

To create some separation between the text you just imported and the Monthly Specials section on the right of the page, you will use the Line tool to draw a line.

1) Choose the Line tool from the Tools panel.

LINE TOOL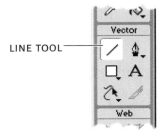

2) Hold down Shift as you drag to draw a vertical line to the left of the month text.

Holding down Shift constrains the line to a vertical, horizontal, or 45-degree-angle line as you drag.

USING THE SUBSELECTION TOOL

How long did you draw the line? Let's say you want the line to be as long as the month text block. To get it right, you could delete the line you just drew and draw it again. However, you can also modify the length of the existing line. When you select the line (or any vector object) with the Pointer tool, you see the anchor points on the path. (A path is two or more connected points; the line you just drew has two connected points.) You can move the line with the Pointer tool, but you can't select the points. To select the points, you need to use the Subselection tool.

1) Choose the Subselection tool on the Tools panel.

The Subselection tool is for selecting objects within a group or selecting points on a path.

SUBSELECTION TOOL

◎ POWER TIP *Instead of switching from the Pointer tool to the Subselection tool, you can hold down Alt (Windows) or Option (Macintosh) to select a point on a path or to select an object in a group.*

2) Click one of the points on the line.

The selected point is solid; the other point is hollow.

3) Drag the solid point to modify the line.

As you drag the point, you can change not only the length of the line, but you can also change the angle of the line. For this line, you want to change just the length. Hold down Shift as you drag the point to keep the line straight. You can also use the arrow keys to move the point instead of dragging it with the Pointer tool.

TIP *You could also change the length of the line by changing its Height value in the Property inspector. To make the line the same height as the text block, select the month text block and look at its height in the Property inspector; then change the line height to the same number.*

114

4) To give your line more interest, experiment with different types of strokes. For example, choose Fur from the Random stroke category and change the tip size to 3 pixels. Change the stroke color to a dark gray.

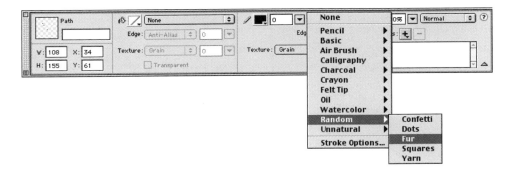

5) Save your file.

You will use this file in a later lesson, but you can close it for now.

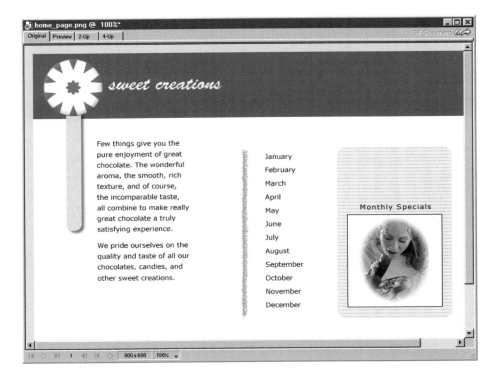

USING PASTE ATTRIBUTES

Fireworks retains the stroke and fill of the last selected object. This means that if you draw a line and change the stroke, then the next line you draw will look the same as the last line. If you switch to the Rectangle tool, then the rectangle you draw will have the same stroke attributes as the previous line. This ability to pick up the attributes of an object is very handy when you want your new objects to have the same look as a previous one.

When you have objects already on the page that you want to look the same, you can use the Paste Attributes command to copy the stroke, fill, and effect from one object to another.

1) Select the object you want to use as the base model and choose Edit > Copy.

Not only are you making a copy of the object, but you are also copying the attributes of the object.

2) Select the object to which you want to copy the attributes and choose Edit > Paste Attributes.

The object takes on the look of the first object. The shape is not changed—only the attributes are copied to this object.

NOTE *The ability to copy and paste attributes from one object to another also works for text. Select a text block and copy it. Then select the next text block and choose Paste Attributes; the formatting from the first text block is applied to the second one.*

WHAT YOU HAVE LEARNED

In this lesson, you have:

- Added text to the page and placed it on a layer [page 102–103]
- Used the formatting controls to change the look of text [pages 104–107]
- Used the spell checker on text [pages 108–109]
- Imported text [page 110]
- Used the Text Editor to change or format text [pages 111–112]
- Used the Line tool and the Subselection tool [pages 113–115]
- Copied the attributes of an object and then pasted them onto another object [page 116]

advanced
techniques

In previous lessons, you built a Web page using some of the basic drawing tools such as the Ellipse and Rectangle tools. In this lesson, you will use path operations, such as Punch and Union, to create more complex objects quickly and easily.

In addition, you will draw and modify a curved path and then add text that curves along the path. You will create some elements for this lesson that you will import to another Web page in another lesson.

In this lesson, you will learn to draw objects such as the ones pictured here.

WHAT YOU WILL LEARN

In this lesson, you will:

- Combine simple shapes into complex objects
- Use techniques for saving and duplicating your actions
- Create a gradient
- Change the opacity of an object
- Add text to a path
- Convert text to a path

APPROXIMATE TIME

This lesson takes approximately 2 hours to complete.

LESSON FILES

Media Files:

None

Starting Files:

None

Completed Projects:

Lesson05\Completed\CD.png

Lesson05\Completed\guitar.png

Lesson05\Completed\clipboard.png

COMBINING SHAPES

A powerful feature in Fireworks is the set of path commands for automating path-drawing tasks that would be difficult, if not impossible, to accomplish manually. The commands, found on the Modify > Combine Paths menu, help you create shapes that you might not be able to create by hand. They also save you time, regardless of your drawing abilities.

In this exercise, you will draw a guitar (acoustic, not electric) for a music page on your Web site. Look at the shape of the guitar in the sample illustration. The curves of the body of the guitar would be difficult to draw, but if you look closely, its body could be created by combining two ovals.

1) Create a new page 400 by 400 pixels with a white canvas. Save the document as *guitar.png* **in the Lesson05 folder.**

This is an example of the finished guitar you will draw in this lesson.

2) Choose View > Rulers; drag a vertical guide to the middle of the canvas and drag a horizontal guide to the bottom third of the canvas.

You will use the guides to help you place the objects that will be used to create the guitar.

3) Select the Ellipse tool from the Tools panel and draw an oval shape. Place the ellipse pointer on the center of the guides and hold down Alt (Windows) or Option (Macintosh) as you drag to draw the oval from the center out. Repeat the process to draw another oval above the first one.

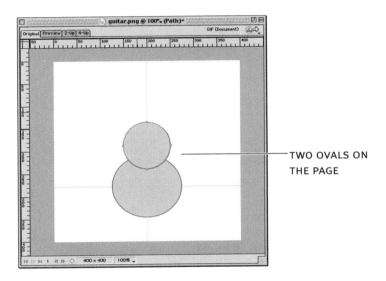

TWO OVALS ON
THE PAGE

The ovals combined form the body of the guitar. If you need to change either oval shape, select the Scale tool and resize or modify the oval. Make sure the two ovals overlap.

4) Select both ovals and then choose Modify > Combine Paths > Union.

The two shapes are combined into one.

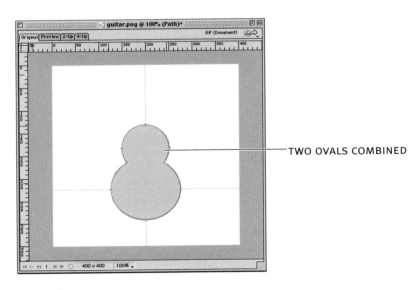

TWO OVALS COMBINED

121

5) Draw a tall, thin rectangle for the neck of the guitar.

Again, if you place the pointer on the vertical guide and hold down Alt (Windows) or Option (Macintosh) as you drag, the rectangle will be centered with the base shape you just created. You can always move the rectangle later if you choose not to use this method. Make sure the bottom of the rectangle overlaps the body of the guitar.

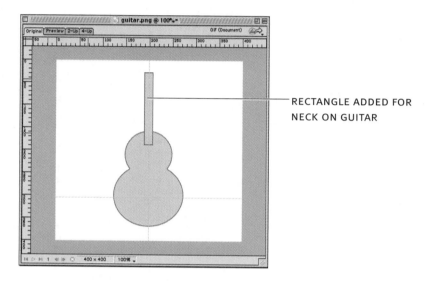

RECTANGLE ADDED FOR
NECK ON GUITAR

6) Combine the rectangle with the base of the guitar as you did in step 4.

Your object should now look like the basic shape of a guitar.

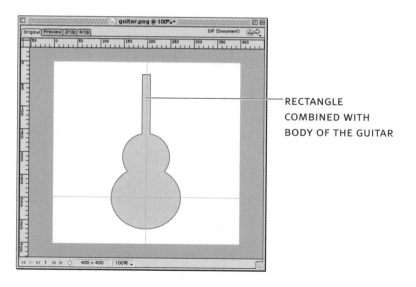

RECTANGLE
COMBINED WITH
BODY OF THE GUITAR

7) Change the color of the guitar to brown and add an inner bevel effect with a smooth edge.

You can pick color number 8 from the basic_colors.png file in the Lesson03 folder for the brown color of the guitar, or pick your own color. Adjust the inner bevel settings to create a smooth, rounded edge around the shape of the guitar.

8) Draw another oval for the center hole in the guitar. Change the color of the center oval to a dark gray and then add an Inset Emboss effect.

Did you remember to draw from the center out using the guides? If not, you can align the oval to the center of the guitar body with the Align commands you used in Lesson 3.

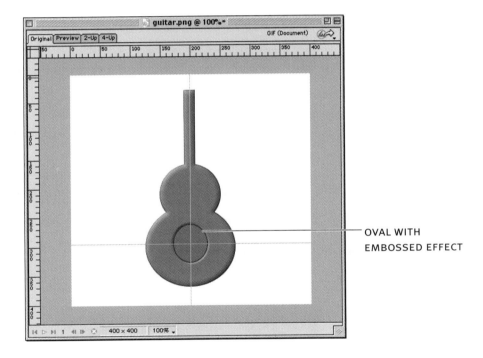

OVAL WITH
EMBOSSED EFFECT

NOTE *In the Inset Emboss window, Show Object is selected by default. With the option selected, the oval remains gray. If you deselect Show Object, the oval turns a darker brown color.*

SHOW
OBJECT IN
EMBOSS
WINDOW

DUPLICATING OBJECTS WITH THE REPEAT COMMAND

Many times you will find yourself creating copies of an object on a page. For example, if you are creating buttons, you might want them all to be the same size and color, with only the text label different. You also might want them aligned and offset the same amount from one another. Once you've created the first one, you can use Copy and Paste, Duplicate, or Clone, or you can hold down Alt (Windows) or Option (Macintosh) and drag to create the remaining buttons.

Although each of these methods results in another object, they all work differently. Using Copy and Paste or Clone puts the duplicate object directly on top of the first, and Duplicate offsets the copy down and to the right. You then have to move the copy to the new location and repeat the process for each new button you want. Then you have to use the alignment commands to make sure that the objects are properly aligned and spaced. When you hold down Alt (Windows) or Option (Macintosh) and drag, the new button is moved, but you must guess the placement and will still need to check the alignment and spacing. The Repeat command makes this process easier.

This exercise demonstrates how to use the Repeat command to repeat a duplicate-and-move process. The Duplicate command duplicates an object, offsetting the new object. This method lets you control the offsetting distance for each new object you create.

1) Draw a small horizontal rectangle at the top of the guitar neck for the tuning keys.

Size and move the rectangle if necessary so it looks proportional to the guitar.

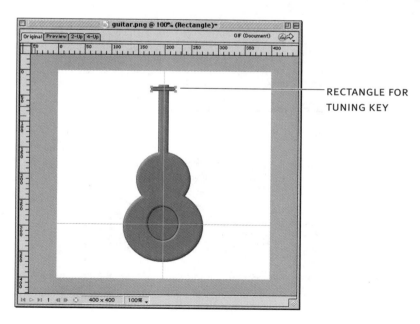

RECTANGLE FOR
TUNING KEY

2) Select the rectangle with the Pointer tool and then hold down Alt (Windows) or Option (Macintosh) as you drag to create a copy of the rectangle. Add Shift as you drag to constrain the copy.

As you drag, the pointer adds a plus sign, indicating that you are making a copy. You actually are performing two operations: you are making a copy, and you are moving the copy a set distance from the original. This method of making a copy is the only one that combines two events in one action. Adding Shift as you drag constrains your movement to a vertical line.

3) Choose Edit > Repeat Duplicate.

Another rectangle is created for you and offset the same distance as the moved object.

The Repeat command repeats the last action. Holding Alt or Option and dragging to make a copy is one action that does two things: it both copies and moves an object. If you use the other copy methods, the Repeat command repeats only the last action, which is the move.

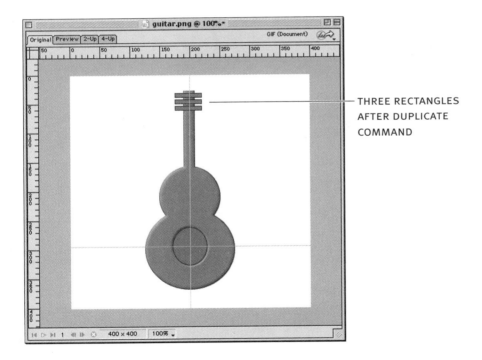

THREE RECTANGLES
AFTER DUPLICATE
COMMAND

4) Draw a vertical line with the Line tool for one of the strings on the guitar. Make the line a 1-point Hard Pencil, with a light gray color. Hold down Shift as you draw the line to constrain the line to a vertical line. Start at the top tuning key and drag below the oval of the center of the guitar.

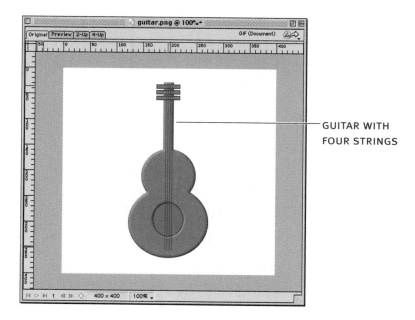

GUITAR WITH
FOUR STRINGS

5) Use the Alt or Option method to make a copy of the line for the next string.

If you feel the line "snap" as you drag, you may have Snap to Guides turned on, which will make it difficult to place the line in the exact location you want. Choose View > Guides > Snap to Guides to deselect the option. Selecting the command toggles the option off and on. If a check is next to the command, it is turned on. If the command does not have a check, the option is off.

6) Use the Repeat command to create a total of four lines for the strings of the guitar.

Guitars actually have six strings, but this stylized version of a guitar is too small for six strings. If it bothers you, you can delete one on the tuning keys to match the number of strings. Yours will be a tenor ukulele or bass guitar instead.

The four strings you just created may not be centered within the neck of the guitar (or ukulele), and you need to position them in the center. If the lines were on their own layer, they would be easy to select. You did create a new layer—right? No problem; you can create one now and easily move the strings onto that layer.

7) Create a new layer and name it *Strings*.

Look on the previous layer. It is called Layer 1 unless you changed the name. The last objects you drew were the four strings. They will be in the top four objects in the layer and identified with the word *Path*.

8) Hold down Shift and click each string object stack.

All the objects are selected on the layer. Look on Layer 1 and you'll see a blue square to the right of the layer name. This is the selection indicator.

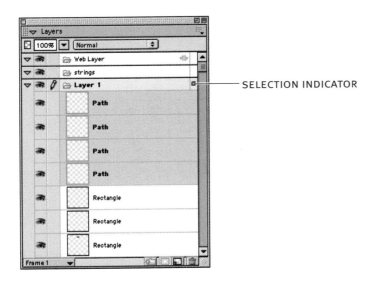

SELECTION INDICATOR

9) Drag the selection indicator from Layer 1 to the String layer.

The four objects are moved to the Strings layer. You could have moved each object one by one to the new layer, but this method is faster. You can use the selection indicator to move one item to a new layer or multiple items as you did in the previous step.

Now with the strings on their own layer, it is easy to select the strings. Once they are in place, you can lock the layer to prevent the strings from moving.

10) Select the four strings and group them. Then select both the string group and the guitar. Choose Modify > Align > Center Vertical to center the strings within the neck of the guitar.

> **NOTE** *If you don't group the strings and you align them using Center Vertical, all strings are stacked one on top of another in the center of the guitar neck. Grouping them centers them as a single item.*

11) Draw a small rectangle at the bottom of the strings.

The rectangle is the bridge that attaches the strings to the base of the guitar.

12) Select all the elements of the guitar and rotate them. Save and close your file.

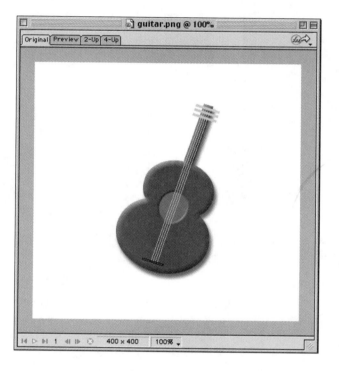

CREATING A CD

The next object to create is a CD for your music page. It will help to look at a CD as you complete this exercise. Rotate the CD slightly and look at the surface as it catches the light. The shimmery surface is the look you are trying to re-create in this exercise. To create the CD, you will draw several concentric circles. You will use the technique you learned in Lesson 2 to draw objects from the center out using guides.

1) Create a new document 400 by 400 pixels with a white canvas. Save the document as *CD.png* in the Lesson05 folder. Choose View > Rulers and drag guides from the top and left rulers. Place the guides in the center of the canvas.

You will use the guides to help you draw several circles aligned to their centers.

2) Click the Default Colors button on the Tools panel and then draw a circle using the guides as the center point of the circle.

The first circle is the CD, so don't draw it too small. Look in the Property inspector once you draw the circle; you want the circle about 250 pixels in diameter.

3) Draw two more circles within this first circle.

If you are looking at a CD, one of these circles will be where the surface of the CD ends, and the other will be the center hole of the CD. Draw the middle circle first (about 100 pixels in diameter) and then the smaller circle (about 30 pixels in diameter).

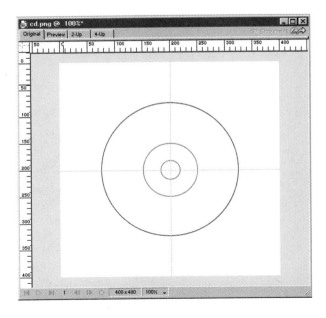

4) Select all three circles and then choose Modify › Combine Paths › Punch.

The last object that you drew (the smaller center hole in this example) cuts (or punches) through the other two circles. If you placed a solid-colored object underneath these circles, you would see the color through the hole.

5) Select the middle circle and change its fill color to a light gray.

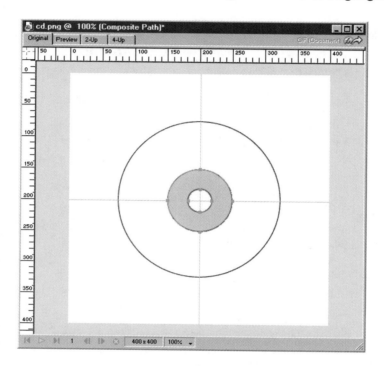

ADDING A GRADIENT

To create the surface of the CD, you will fill the larger circle with a gradient. Gradients are schemes in which colors gradually blend from one to another to create a smooth color transition. A gradient must have at least two colors defined, but you can define as many colors as you want and change the angle that the gradient follows.

1) Select the larger circle. Choose Cone from the Fill category pop-up menu in the Property inspector.

The center section of the Fill category pop-up menu contains the various gradient fills you can use. Later you might want to experiment with these different looks. The Cone gradient creates the appearance of looking down on a cone shape. Because you "punched" a hole in the center of your circle, you don't see the tip of the cone on your circle. You should see the color variation in the circle using the default colors of black and white.

You can edit the gradient to change the colors and the angle of the blend. Look at your circle. You'll see a black horizontal line, with a circle handle on one end and a square handle on the other. The circle handle indicates the starting point of the gradient. (On a Radial or Cone gradient, the circle represents the center of the gradient.) The square handle controls the width of the gradient.

NOTE *The black horizontal line is difficult to see over the black portion of the gradient, but you should be able to see it in the middle of the circle. If not, turn off the ruler guides.*

2) Move the pointer over the line. Drag the line when you see a circular arrow.

The angle of the gradient changes based on the angle of the line.

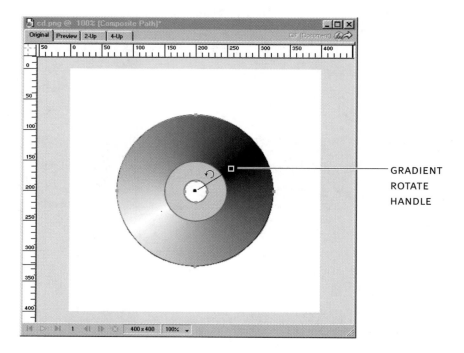

GRADIENT
ROTATE
HANDLE

3) Drag the circle handle away from the center of the circle.

The circle is the center point of the gradient, or the tip of the cone in this gradient. When you move the circle handle away from the center, you now see the tip that was hidden in the punched hole.

4) Drag the square handle to change the width of the gradient.

Move the square handle close to the circle handle and then away to see what happens. With this gradient, the change is minimal. With other gradient types, such as a Linear gradient, you will see results that are more dramatic when you adjust these handles.

NOTE *With a Linear gradient, when you move the square handle away from the object, more of the top color is visible in the gradient. When you drag the square handle closer to the circle handle, more of the bottom color is visible.*

5) Double-click either handle of the gradient.

For this gradient, you want the circle and square handles returned to their default positions. You could move them individually, but double-clicking is quicker. The shortcut is a double-click on either handle.

6) Click the Fill color box in the Property inspector.

The Fill panel opens to the gradient editing window, displaying the color swatches, a color ramp, and a preview ramp. Here you can change the colors in your gradient or use the preset gradients.

You drag a color swatch to change the amount of a color in the gradient. The color ramp displays a preview of the final gradient. You click one of the color swatches to change the color and then choose a color from the color palette. You see this same palette in all the color boxes. You can choose one of the color chips on the palette or use the Options menu to switch to another color palette.

If you want more than two colors in your gradient, click the gray area under the first ramp. Drag to move this new color swatch or click to change its color. To delete a color swatch, drag it off the editing window.

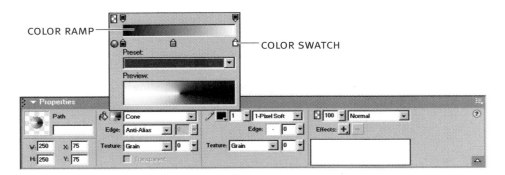

7) Choose Silver from the Preset gradients pop-up menu. When you finish editing the gradient, click outside the gradient editing window to close it.

If you made any change to the colors in the gradient, they are replaced by these new colors and color swatches. Your CD should now have that shimmering look. Look at the color swatches to see how this effect was accomplished. It looks good, but it has little color.

8) To add some color to the CD, choose Pastels from the Preset gradients pop-up menu. Press Enter (Windows) or Return (Macintosh) to close the Edit Gradient window.

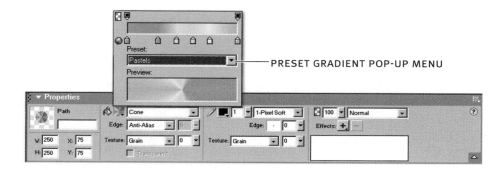

PRESET GRADIENT POP-UP MENU

9) Set the stroke to None from the Stroke category pop-up menu in the Property inspector.

Now the CD is taking shape.

CHANGING THE OPACITY

Look at the gray inner circle in your CD. The circle is a solid color; you cannot see the pastel color of the circle beneath it. By changing the opacity of the circle, you can control the amount of transparency in the fill.

1) Select the gray middle circle and then drag the Opacity slider in the Property inspector to 50 percent.

OPACITY SLIDER

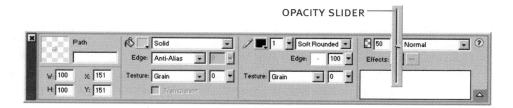

You can experiment with the percentage amount and set it to your liking. You want the pastel colors of the larger circle to show through the middle circle. If you are looking at a CD, this middle section is actually transparent, but adding a little color gives it more interest.

The CD is almost complete. Look again at a CD, to see the outside edge that reflects the depth of the CD. To create this edge, you will draw another circle and add a beveled effect.

134

2) Draw another circle from the center out and make it slightly larger than the pastel circle. Change the fill color of this circle to dark gray.

Fireworks retains the stroke and fill of the last selected object (in this example, the gray circle) and uses those settings for the next object you draw.

The circle is on top of the other circles and needs to be moved to the back. There are several ways you can move the top circle. You can choose Modify > Arrange > Send to Back, or you can use the Modify toolbar (in Windows only). You can also use the Layers panel to change the stacking order of objects.

3) On the Layers panel, drag the object for the circle (it's labeled Path) below the other two objects on the layer.

You'll see a black (or double) line as you drag that indicates the position of the object. Release the mouse button when the black line is below the last object on the layer. The circle is now placed beneath the other circle.

NOTE *The other two circles are labeled Composite Path on the Layers panel. A composite path is created when you combine two paths. When you used the Punch command, you combined the larger circle with the smaller circle, creating a composite path.*

4) Click the eye icons on the Layers panel to hide the two circles that are now on top of the gray circle.

Using the Layers panel to selectively hide and show layers or object stacks makes working on a single object easy.

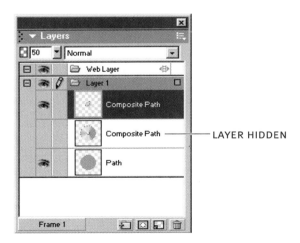

135

5) Select the gray circle and add an Inner Bevel effect. Click outside the settings window to close it and then click the eye icons again on the Layers panel to see the other circles.

You can leave the bevel settings at the defaults. Once you display the other circles, can you see a problem? The hole for the CD is now covered with the bottom circle.

6) You need to punch another hole in the bottom circle. Again, hide the top two circles so you can see only the gray bottom circle. Draw another circle and then repeat the steps as you did before to punch this circle in the gray circle.

Make sure that the new circle you draw is as large or larger than the middle circle; otherwise, you will see it through the hole in the CD. Display the other circles, and your CD is complete.

7) Save your file.

ADDING TEXT ALONG A PATH

The CD looks good, but it's blank, and you want to add a label. Instead of placing text horizontally on the CD, you decide to rotate it around the circle. To do that, you will draw another circle (you should have circles perfected by now!) and have your text follow along the outline of the circle.

1) Add a new layer and name it *Text*. Draw a circle on this layer, using the guides to draw from the center.

The text will sit on this circle, so you want it centered within the CD. The fill and stroke of this circle can be anything—they won't show after you attach the text.

2) Select the Text tool, click outside the circle, and type *Smooth Jazz*.

It doesn't matter where you place the text for this step.

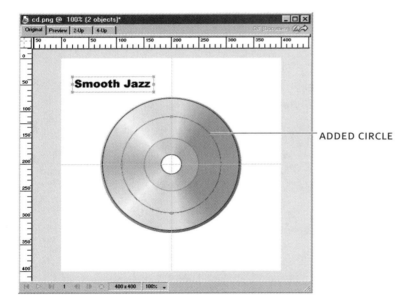

ADDED CIRCLE

3) Format the text as Arial Black, 20 points.

You can change these settings to your liking after the next step.

4) Select both the text and the last circle; then choose Text > Attach to Path.

TIP *The easiest way to select the circle is to select its object stack on the Layers panel.*

137

The text is placed around the circle and remains completely editable. Make any changes to the text to make it easier to read. For example, text curved around the circle may cause some of the characters to touch. Use the Range Kerning controls to increase the spacing. If you want to increase the spacing only between two letters, place the insertion bar between the two letters and adjust the kerning.

The baseline of the text is attached to the path. To change the text after it is attached to the path, double-click the text to change to text editing mode. If you want to detach the text from the path, choose Text > Detach from Path.

TIP *You can also edit the text using the Text Editor, which may be easier since the text is along a curve. Choose Text > Editor to open the Text Editor. Make your changes and then click OK to exit the Text Editor.*

Several options control how the text flows on the path. For a curved path, the placement on the path logically follows the alignment: left-aligned text starts at the beginning of the path; right-aligned text ends at the end of the path.

If your path is a circle as is the case here, the text flow is a bit more confusing. A circle consists of four anchor points: top, bottom, left, and right. The path of the circle flows clockwise, with the beginning point at 9 o'clock. Text is aligned on the circle based on the beginning anchor point.

Notice that your text begins at the left side of the circle—at 9 o'clock. Click Center Alignment in the Property inspector to change the text alignment. Your text moves to 3 o'clock. That may not be what you expected, or what you wanted. Click Left Alignment to reset the text.

5) Type *15* in the Text Offset text box in the Property inspector.

The Text Offset value shifts text on the path the specified number of pixels in the direction of the path. If you enter a positive number, the text shifts clockwise. If you enter a negative number, the text shifts counterclockwise.

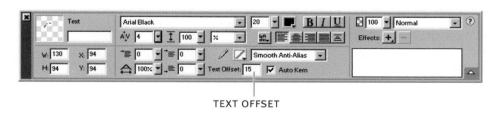

TEXT OFFSET

You might also want to experiment with the orientation of the text to the path. Choose Text > Orientation and choose Rotate Around Path, Vertical, Skew Vertical, or Skew Horizontal.

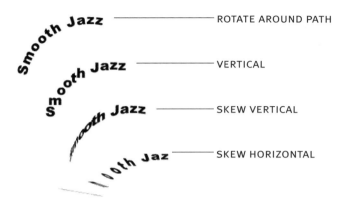

ROTATE AROUND PATH

VERTICAL

SKEW VERTICAL

SKEW HORIZONTAL

- **Rotate Around Path** is the default. Each letter is placed perpendicular to the path.
- **Vertical** positions each letter vertical to the page.
- **Skew Vertical** rotates the letters on the path, but skews them vertically.
- **Skew Horizontal** slants the letters horizontally based on the curve of the path.

6) Once you have the text to your liking, save and close the file.

You will import both the guitar and the CD to a Web page in another lesson.

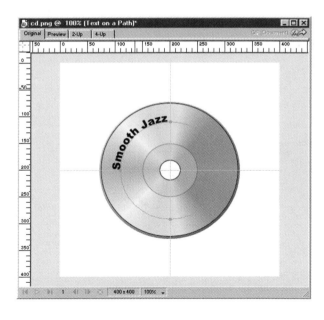

USING THE INTERSECT AND CROP COMMANDS

In this lesson, you learned two of the Combine Paths commands: Union and Punch. The other two—Intersect and Crop—are not needed in this lesson, but you may want to experiment with them in a new document to see what results you get. Draw two shapes, placing the last shape on top of the first. For example, draw a circle on a vertical rectangle. Select both shapes and choose Modify > Combine Paths > Intersect. The area of the paths that is common to both objects is converted to a single path, and the nonoverlapping areas are removed.

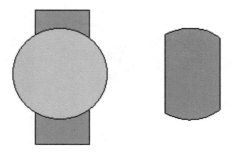

The Crop command is a bit more difficult to visualize. Draw two or more shapes with the Rectangle, Polygon, and Ellipse tools. On top of all the objects, position the object that you want to use as the cropping shape. Select all of the objects by holding down Shift and clicking each object with the Pointer tool. Choose Modify > Combine Paths > Crop.

The bottom path is altered by the shape of the topmost path so that its area under the top path is removed. This could result in an altered simple path shape or a compound path, depending on the location and nature of the top path.

NOTE *Crop is the opposite of Punch. Whereas Punch removes the area inside of the top object, Crop removes the area outside of the top object.*

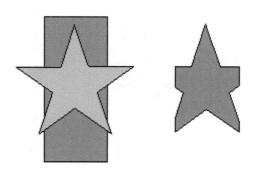

CONVERTING TEXT TO PATHS

When you use the Text tool, you create editable text. That means that you can change the font, size, and color of the text or change the text itself. There are occasions when you might want to work with the text as if it were a graphic element. To do that, you convert the text to a path. Converting text to paths changes the text outline to a graphic object; the text can no longer be edited as text. However, after conversion, you can alter the look of the text shape by moving or reshaping the path.

1) Select the Text tool and type some text on the page—for example, type *Smooth Jazz* as you did in the last exercise. Choose a font and point size.

For the font, choose an unusual typeface you might have on your computer and use a large point size such as 64 points.

2) Choose Text > Convert to Paths.

The text is converted to a graphic. The look of the text on the screen should not change, but four corner handles should appear. All of the converted characters are grouped together. If you want to work with individual characters, choose Modify > Ungroup to ungroup the paths. If you want to work with the text as a single composite path, choose Modify > Combine Paths > Join.

In the next exercise, you will use the text graphic and change its shape and orientation.

smooth jazz ——— TEXT CONVERTED TO PATHS AND UNGROUPED

smooth jazz ——— TEXT CONVERTED TO PATHS AND MODIFIED

APPLYING TRANSFORMATIONS

Fireworks provides several commands and tools you can use to scale, rotate, distort, and skew an object, a group of objects, or a pixel selection area. These actions are called transformations. You can use the transform tools on the Tools panel, or you can choose Modify > Transform and pick an option from the submenu. When you choose a tool or Transform menu item, the selected item displays transform handles. Drag any transform handle to edit the object. You used the Scale and Rotate tools in a previous lesson; in this exercise, you will use the Skew and Distort tools.

1) Select your text graphic and choose the Skew tool, or choose Modify › Transform › Skew.

Skewing an object transforms it by slanting it along the horizontal or vertical axis, or both axes. You can skew an object by dragging one of the transform handles, dragging inward or outward.

2) Place the pointer over any handle. Drag the handle to change the angles or side lengths of the object. Hold down Shift to constrain the skewing proportionally. Double-click the object or press Enter (Windows) or Return (Macintosh) to apply the transformation.

SKEW HANDLES

142

3) With your text object still selected, choose the Distort tool, or choose Modify ›
Transform › Distort.

The Distort tool allows you to change the proportions of the object by dragging any transform handle. Unlike with the Skew tool, you can control each handle individually.

NOTE *Although you are using the text you converted to paths, it is not necessary to do so to apply transformations. You can transform normal text and keep it editable.*

4) Place the pointer over any handle. Drag the handle to change the shape of the object. Double-click the object or press Enter (Windows) or Return (Macintosh) to apply the transformation.

You don't need to save this file with your experiments.

ON YOUR OWN

To practice what you've learned, try drawing a clipboard as shown here. Create three layers, one for each main element of the clipboard: the board, the pad, and the clip. For the colors of the clipboard objects, you can look at the clipboard.png file in the Lesson05 Completed folder, or be creative and pick your own colors.

Hints: Use the Repeat command to draw the lines on the pad. Combine shapes (rectangles and rounded rectangles) for the clip and punch the hole in the clip with a circle. Add a gradient to the clip to add some dimension.

144

WHAT YOU HAVE LEARNED

In this lesson, you have:

- Combined simple shapes to draw the body of a guitar [pages 120–123]
- Used the Repeat command to draw the strings of a guitar [pages 124–128]
- Added a gradient to add dimension to a CD [pages 129–134]
- Changed the opacity of an object [pages 134–136]
- Added text along a path [pages 137–140]
- Used the Intersect and Crop commands [page 140]
- Converted text to paths [page 141]
- Used the Skew and Distort tools [pages 142–143]

creating buttons

LESSON 6

As you design your Web site, you may want to create buttons to add interest and interactivity to your pages. The buttons you make can be simple rectangles with the name of the link or 3D buttons that react to the mouse by changing color, glowing, or taking on the look of a mechanical button that has been pressed down.

In Fireworks MX, you can create a variety of buttons, complete with all the JavaScript and HTML that make them work. You can create simple buttons, and you can use the Button Editor; you can even create your own custom buttons that you can save to use again.

A rollover is an image that changes appearance when the user moves the pointer over it or clicks it. There are four common button states, although you can choose to use only two or three states if you prefer. Each state reflects the user's interaction

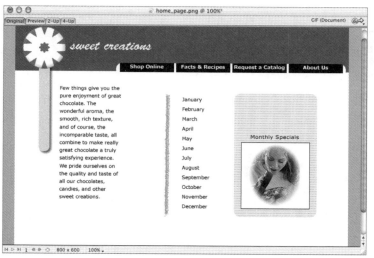

In this lesson, you will use the Button Editor to create buttons, then place them on the home page you are creating.

with the button: when the user moves the mouse pointer over the image, when the user moves the mouse pointer away from the image, when the user clicks the image, and when the user moves the mouse pointer over a clicked button (the down state of a button).

First, you create each of the different looks of the image; then Fireworks creates the HTML and JavaScript needed to make the rollover work in your browser. Fireworks uses frames to store the individual images for the different states of the rollover. The Up state image goes in frame 1, the Over state image goes in frame 2, the Down state image goes in frame 3, and the OverWhileDown state image goes in frame 4.

WHAT YOU WILL LEARN

In this lesson, you will:

- Use the Button Editor to create buttons
- Add a new button from an existing button
- Make changes to the button
- Add links to your buttons
- Turn graphics into buttons

APPROXIMATE TIME

This lesson takes approximately 1 hour to complete.

LESSON FILES

Media Files:
None

Starting Files:
Lesson06\Start\home_page_L6.png

Completed Projects:
Lesson06\Completed\buttons.png
Lesson06\Completed\home_page_L6.png

USING THE BUTTON EDITOR

The Button Editor steps you through the process of creating all states of a button and adding the links and HTML to make everything work. Most of the time, you'll want to use this editor, but you can still create buttons manually if you prefer. When you use the Button Editor, the button is added to the library. This makes adding other buttons of the same type a snap—you just drag the new button from the library onto the canvas.

Most often, you'll create simple rollovers for your buttons. A simple rollover switches to a new image when the user rolls the pointer over the button and then switches back as the user rolls the pointer off the image. A simple rollover requires only two graphics, making downloading fast. The next exercise shows you how to create a three-state button using the Button Editor.

1) Create a new document 600 by 300 pixels with a white canvas. Save your file in the Lesson06 folder and name it *buttons.png*. Choose Edit > Insert > New Button to access the Button Editor.

The Button Editor is a separate window where you design your button. All of the tools and panels are available just as they are in the standard document window.

2) Draw a rectangle in the Button Editor window. Make the width of the rectangle 130 pixels and the height 30 pixels. Change the Fill color to black and change the Stroke to None.

Notice the five tabs at the top of the Editor. The Up tab is where you create the normal state of your button. The normal state is the look of the button as it initially appears on the page.

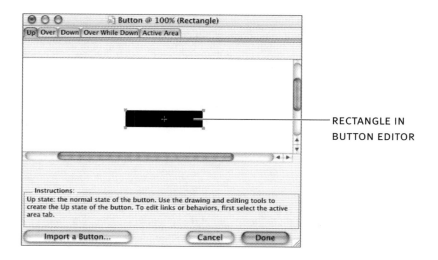

RECTANGLE IN
BUTTON EDITOR

3) Use the Text tool to add the label *Shop Online* to the button.

Place the text block in the center of the rectangle. Change the text color to white and set the alignment to centered. Choose a font and size of your liking (for example Verdana, 12 points), leaving some room on either side of the text. Align the text block so that it is centered between the left and right edges of the rectangle. Move the text block closer to the bottom edge.

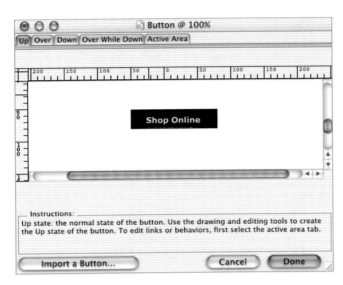

NOTE *For the other buttons on the page, you will copy the completed button and then change the text label. The other buttons are labeled Facts & Recipes, Request a Catalog, and About Us. If your text block is centered in the rectangle and the text alignment set to Centered, then when you change the text labels on the other buttons, the text block expands or contracts based on the text, but remains centered in the rectangle.*

If you are not pleased with your button, adjust it now. The other states of the button are based on this state. Although you can adjust the button later, it is much easier if you make your adjustments now. You know: get it right the first time!

4) Select the Over tab to create the rollover image. Click Copy Up Graphic to make a copy of the original button (the rectangle and the text) you just created. Select the rectangle and change the color to gray.

The button you created in the Up window is copied and pasted in the exact location in the Over window. Normally, the rollover image is based on the original image, with perhaps just the color of the text or shade of the button changed.

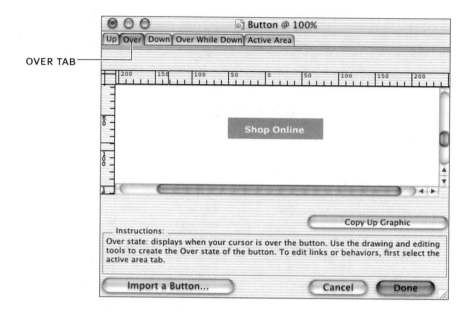

5) Select the Down tab to create the image that is displayed when the user clicks the button. Click Copy Over Graphic to make a copy of the previous state of the button. Select the rectangle and change the color to the same red color you added to the top rectangle on your home_page.png file.

If you don't remember the same red color you used, you can open the basic_colors.png file in the Lesson03 folder and pick the color from the first color chip. Or open your home_page.png file and pick the color from the top rectangle. You can open either of these files while the Button Editor is open.

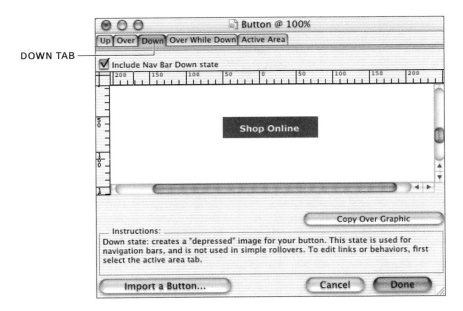

6) Click Done to exit the Button Editor.

When you exit the Button Editor, you are returned to the document window. The button is placed in the center of the canvas, but you can move it wherever you want. For this exercise, move the button to the left of the canvas. Your button is visible, and you see a green translucent overlay (called a slice) and the red slice guide lines.

Up to this point, you've created static images on the page. The button you just created includes some JavaScript that instructs the browser to change the image from the Up state to the Over state when the user moves over the button and to change to the Down state when the user clicks the button. Fireworks did all that work for you and stored the code in the slice. The slice is placed on the Web Layer and is always on top.

7) If the slice guides are not visible, choose View > Slice Guides to display them. If the slice is not visible, click Show Slices and Hotspots on the Tools panel to show it.

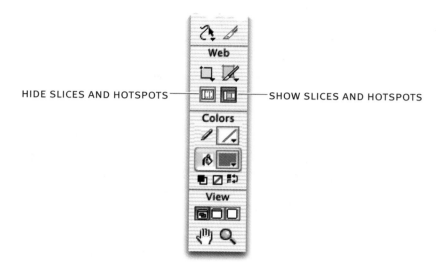

HIDE SLICES AND HOTSPOTS ——— ——— SHOW SLICES AND HOTSPOTS

The slices and slice guides are very helpful for placing other buttons on the page relative to this first one, but they can be distracting. You will find yourself showing them and then hiding them as you design your page. Hide them for the next task.

TIP *Clicking Show or Hide Slices on the Tools panel is the same as hiding or showing the Web Layer on the Layers panel.*

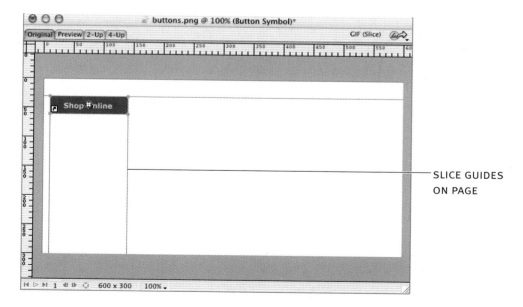

SLICE GUIDES
ON PAGE

152

8) Select the Preview tab in the document window to view your button.

Move the pointer over the button to see the rollover image. The button changes to the Over state and then returns to the Up state when you move off the button. Click the button to see the Down state of the button.

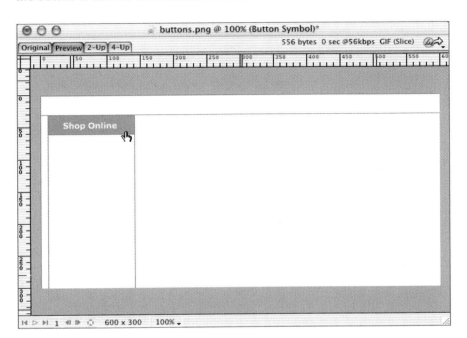

NOTE *At this point, you have only one button. Once you click the button, it remains in the Down state. If you have two or more buttons, then the clicked button returns to the Up state when you click another button. This type of button interaction is referred to as a Nav Bar as opposed to a simple rollover.*

9) Select the Original tab to return to the document window.

TIP *You cannot edit the button while you are in the Preview window. You must return to the original document window to make your changes.*

ADDING A NEW BUTTON

The Button Editor added your button to the library as a symbol named Button. Symbols are objects or groups of objects that you use when you want to control multiple copies of objects. Copies of the symbol are referred to as instances. In this case, you want several buttons to look the same, only with different text.

1) Choose Window > Library to view your button in the library.

The Library panel is docked within the Assets panel group. You could also click the disclosure triangle in the Assets panel group and then click the Library tab.

LIBRARY TAB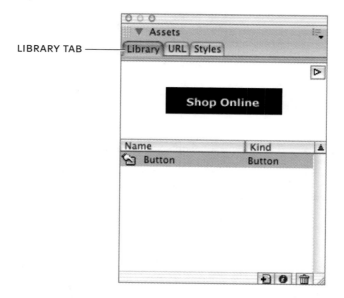

In the library, in the Preview pane, you see the button you just created, and you see the button name (Button in this example) in the Library list. For this exercise, you will have only the one button, but there may be times when you have multiple buttons that you want to name.

2) Double-click the name in the list. In the Symbol Properties dialog box, type a descriptive name and then click OK.

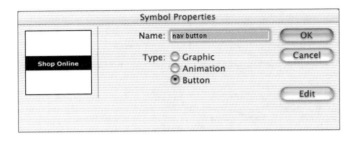

3) Drag the button name from the Library list to the page.

A copy of the button (an instance) is placed on the page. Move the copy of the button to the right of the first button.

> **TIP** *You can drag either the button name or the button image from the Preview pane to place a copy on the page.*

4) Drag two more copies of the button to the page, moving each one to the right of the last button.

You now have four buttons, all with the same name. You'll change the names in step 6.

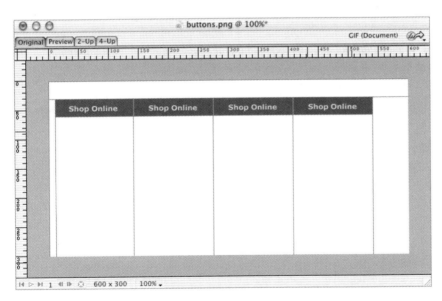

5) Select all of the buttons. Choose Window › Align and then click the Align Top Edge icon on the panel to align all of the buttons along their top edges. Then click Space Evenly Horizontally on the Align panel to space the buttons equally from one another.

Make sure that the To Canvas button in the Align panel is not selected; otherwise, your buttons will align to the top of the canvas rather than aligning to their top edges.

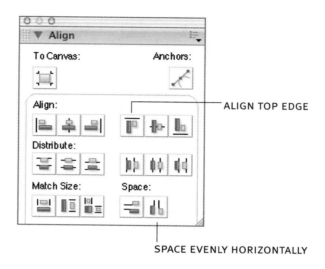

ALIGN TOP EDGE

SPACE EVENLY HORIZONTALLY

If Snap to Guides is on, your buttons snap in place when you drag them on the page. If so, this step to align the buttons is not necessary.

TIP *If you want your buttons to touch on the sides, you'll need to manually move then together. You can use the arrow keys to nudge your buttons.*

NOTE *Fireworks MX contains a special Macromedia Flash reader that allows SWF files to play as commands and panels within Fireworks. The Align panel is actually a Macromedia Flash movie. If you look in the Configuration > Command Panels folder within your Fireworks application folder, you'll see the align.swf file for the panel.*

6) Select the second button. In the Property inspector, change the text label to
Facts & Recipes **and then press Enter (Windows) or Return (Macintosh).**

The text on the second button is changed without affecting the text on the first button.

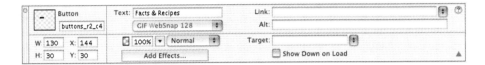

7) Repeat step 6 for the two remaining buttons, changing the text to *Request a*
Catalog **and** *About Us*, **respectively. Save your file and then check your buttons in**
the Preview window.

When the pointer is over a button, it changes color. When you click a button, it
changes to the Down state. When you click another button, the first button returns
to its normal state.

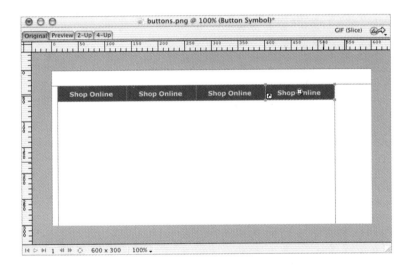

CHANGING YOUR BUTTONS

The last three buttons you created are copies (or instances) of the first button you
created. If you use Macromedia Flash, you probably are familiar with symbols and
how they work. The principle is much the same in Fireworks. The advantage of a
symbol is the ease of changing the look of the buttons. Say, for example, that you
don't like the color of the buttons when you place them on a Web page. If you had
individual buttons, you would need to select each button and then make the change.
Since your buttons are instances of the same symbol, you just need to change the
original symbol, and then each instance is automatically changed: a real time-saver!

1) Click the Original tab and then double-click any button on the page.

This opens the Button Editor. You can also double-click the button icon or the button image in the Preview pane of the library.

TIP *If you click the name of the button instead of the icon of the button in the Library list, the Symbol Properties dialog box opens instead of the Button Editor. You can then click Edit to open the Button Editor.*

2) Make your change to the button in the Button Editor.

For this example, change the color of the rectangle in the Up state of the button to red.

3) Click Done to close the Button Editor.

All the buttons on the page are now red.

4) Double-click one of the buttons again and reset the rectangle to black.

For this lesson, you want the buttons black.

ADDING A NAME AND A LINK TO BUTTONS

Your buttons may look great, but they are missing an important element. After all, the main purpose of a button is to provide a method of linking to another page of your site. You can add links to your buttons in Fireworks, or you can add them later in Macromedia Dreamweaver. To add a link to a button in Fireworks, select the button and then type the link in the Link text box in the Property inspector. Enter a name for your button in the Button name text box. The name you enter for a button is the name that is assigned to the image when you export your page.

1) Select the Shop Online button and then type *shop.htm* for the link and *shop* for the name; for the Facts & Recipes button, type *facts.htm* for the link and *facts* for the name; for the Request a Catalog button, type *request.htm* for the link and *request* for the name; and for the About Us button, type *about.htm* for the link and *about* for the name.

BUTTON NAME   LINK TEXT BOX

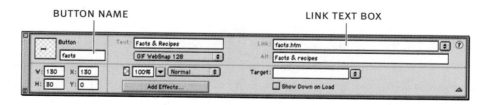

2) Select each button again and type a description of the button in the Alt text box in the Property inspector. For example, type *Shop Online Button* in the Alt text box for the first button, and so on.

Alternate (Alt) text is displayed when the user moves over the button. It is also displayed if the graphics are slow to download, or if the user has turned off graphic display in the browser. Alt text also plays an important role for the visually impaired. Users with screen readers (the computer kind) hear your page spoken. To speak your buttons, the reader uses the Alt text associated with the button. To make your pages accessible to everyone, take the extra time to add Alt text to all of your buttons.

3) Choose Modify › Canvas › Trim Canvas and then save your file.

IMPORTING YOUR BUTTONS

In the next steps, you are going to add your buttons to the home page you created in the earlier lessons. Then you are going to cut out a piece of the red header rectangle and place the buttons under the cutout.

1) Open the home_page.png file you created in Lesson 3 and modified in Lesson 4.

You can use the file home_page_L6.png in the Lesson06 Start folder if you can't find the file you created. If you use this file, choose File > Save As and rename the file home_page.png and save it in the Lesson06 folder.

2) Create a new layer and name it *Buttons*.

The Buttons layer needs to be above the Header layer—its position doesn't matter for the other layers.

3) Choose File > Import and locate the buttons.png file you just created. Click Open. Click the red rectangle to place your buttons.

The buttons are placed on the page. Move them so that the bottom edges of the buttons sit on the bottom right edge of the red rectangle.

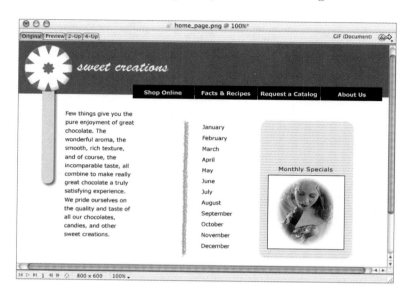

4) Draw a rounded rectangle on top of the buttons.

Set the roundness of the rectangle between 80 and 90. Position the rectangle so that the top edge of the rectangle is at the top edges of the buttons, and the sides of the rectangle overlap the left side of the first button and the right side of the last button.

ROUNDED RECTANGLE PLACED OVER BUTTONS

TIP *Change the fill of the rectangle to None so you can see the buttons as you position the rectangle.*

5) Select the rounded rectangle and the red rectangle.

Be careful not to select any of the buttons when you complete this step.

6) Choose Modify > Combine Paths > Punch.

You now have a portion of the header removed. Your buttons are on top and now need to be moved underneath the Header layer.

7) Drag the Button layer below the Header layer.

Your task is complete. Aren't layers great!

8) Select the red rectangle and add a drop shadow. Save your file.

Your home page is almost complete. In the next lesson, you will add some user interactivity to display the monthly special for your Web site.

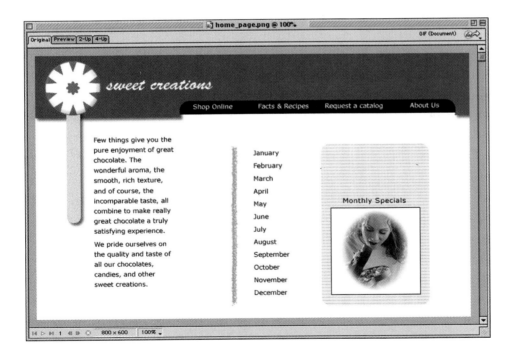

CHANGING GRAPHICS TO BUTTONS

The Button Editor is a tremendous time-saving tool and works great when you first create your buttons as you did in this lesson. You can even use it for graphics already drawn on the page.

When you first design your Web pages, you may want to concentrate on the look of the page and not worry about adding links or making buttons. For example, when the Web page you just completed was designed, the elements were placed on the canvas as graphics. Several ideas for the page were thrown out before the final concept emerged. The buttons were just rectangles with text labels. The rectangles and their text were then converted to buttons to complete the page.

To see how easy this step is, you will create some simple graphics on a page and then convert them to buttons.

1) Create a new document 400 by 400 pixels with a white canvas.

You don't have to save this document. The buttons you create on this page are only experiments.

2) Draw a rectangle or any shape you want for a button and then add some text.

You can get as fancy as you want—add a bevel or a drop shadow.

The object you just added to the page might look like a button, but at this point it is just another graphic element on the page. To make it a button with links and perhaps even a rollover, you need to convert it to a symbol. When you created your button with the Button Editor, the Button Editor automatically converted your objects to symbols. If you don't use the Button Editor, you need to manually convert the elements.

3) Select all the elements for the button. Choose Modify > Symbol > Convert to Symbol. In the Symbol Properties dialog box, give your button a name and then select Button. Click OK.

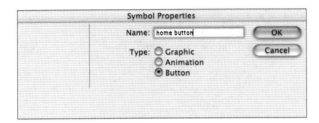

Your objects are now a button symbol, and the button has been added to the library. To add a rollover or make any changes, follow the same steps as described earlier in this lesson in the section "Changing Your Buttons."

You can close this file without saving it.

WHAT YOU HAVE LEARNED

In this lesson, you have:

- Created a rollover button using the Button Editor [pages 148–153]
- Created new buttons from the original and then changed the text and links [pages 154–159]
- Added a name and a link to the buttons [pages 158– 159]
- Imported the buttons to the home page [pages 159–161]
- Converted graphics to a button [pages 162–163]

creating slices and hotspots

The rollover buttons you added to the home page in the previous lesson add some interest to your page. The buttons also provide some feedback to the user. In this lesson, you will learn a variety of techniques to add interactivity to your pages. You will start by creating an image map where the user can click multiple areas of an image to link to other pages of your site. You will further explore the concept of slicing an image, learning to add behaviors to the slice to swap images.

You will add more interactivity to your home page in this lesson by adding disjointed rollovers to the month text.

WHAT YOU WILL LEARN

In this lesson, you will:

- Add hotspots to an image to create an image map

- Work with the Web Layer

- Add slices to your page

- Add frames to the document

- Create disjointed rollovers

- View your page in full-screen mode

APPROXIMATE TIME

This lesson takes approximately 1 hour to complete.

LESSON FILES

Media Files:

Lesson07\Months\january.png
Lesson07\Months\february.png
Lesson07\Months\march.png
Lesson07\Months\april.png
Lesson07\Months\may.png
Lesson07\Months\june.png
Lesson07\Months\july.png
Lesson07\Months\august.png
Lesson07\Months\september.png
Lesson07\Months\october.png
Lesson07\Months\november.png
Lesson07\Months\december.png

Starting Files:

Lesson07\banner.png
Lesson07\home_page_L7.png

Completed Projects:

Lesson07\banner.png
Lesson07\home_page_L7.png

CREATING AN IMAGE MAP

By definition, all of your exported graphics are rectangular. If you make a graphic a link, then the shape of the link is rectangular as well. You can make a portion of a graphic transparent, or make its background color the same color as the background color of the Web page, giving the illusion of a different shape, but you will still have a rectangle. If you want to make a link area a shape other than a rectangle, or if you want to create several links on one image, then you have to use an image map.

For example, suppose you have a map of the world, and you want a link for each country. Most countries have irregular shapes, and none are neatly ordered side by side. You need to distinguish the different shapes of each country and then assign a different link to each shape. This is what an image map does.

The link areas on an image map are referred to as hotspots in Fireworks. A hotspot area on a graphic can be one of three shapes: a rectangle, a circle, or a polygon. The hotspot is an area that is translated to an image map when you export your page to HTML; it is not part of the graphic. The next exercise shows you how to create the hotspots on an image and then assign links to the hotspots.

Although it is easy to create image maps in an HTML editor such as Macromedia Dreamweaver, Macromedia Fireworks can accomplish the same task for you. The resulting HTML can then be pasted into your Web page or inserted into your Dreamweaver project.

1) Open the banner.png file located in the Start folder of the Lesson07 folder.

For this exercise, you want to assign a link to the Web page within a banner and a link to the monthly special.

2) Select the Rectangle Hotspot tool from the Tools panel and draw a rectangle around the Web address. A blue translucent rectangular area (the hotspot) appears.

The size of the hotspot rectangle determines where the user must click to select the link. If you are designing a site for small children, you want the hotspot area large enough for unsteady hands to select. In this exercise, you want the hotspot to cover the text.

After you draw the rectangle, you may need to change its size or move it on the canvas. Make sure that you switch to the Pointer tool to make any changes to the hotspot.

You'll notice a small white marker in the middle of your hotspot area. This marker (called the behavior handle) is for adding behaviors to the hotspot. You'll use this later in the lesson.

3) Hold down on the Hotspot tool to access the Circle Hotspot tool; then draw a circle around the candy.

The hotspot tools work like other vector tools. To draw from the center, hold down Alt (Windows) or Option (Macintosh) as you draw with the tool.

TIP *You do not need to hold down the Shift key as you draw a circle with the Circle Hotspot tool; it always draws a circle.*

4) Use the Polygon Hotspot tool to draw a shape around the candy stick.

The Polygon Hotspot tool works differently than the other tools. Instead of clicking and dragging to draw the shape, just click around the shape. Each time you click, a point on the hotspot is created. Continue to click until you have a hotspot that roughly outlines the area.

After the third point is added, the hotspot area begins to form. Continue to click around the shape. You can add as many points as you want; the more points, the closer the hotspot comes to defining the shape. A point to remember is that your users generally will click on or around the text description within the shape, so your hotspot area just needs to cover most of the area.

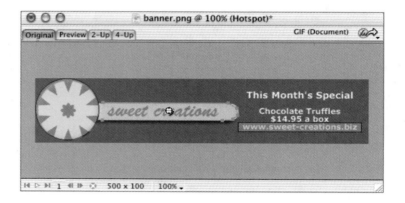

TIP *When drawing your hotspots, make sure you don't overlap an existing hotspot. If you do, the topmost hotspot takes precedence.*

5) Select each hotspot with the Pointer tool. In the Link text box in the Property inspector, type *http://www.sweet-creations.biz* for the Web address, *http://www.sweet-creations.biz/specials* for the candy stick, and *http://www.sweet-creations.biz/candy* for the candy.

Once you have the hotspots on the image, you need to assign a link for each of them. In the Property inspector, you assign the link, Alt text, and a target for the link. (The target generally applies to pages built with frames. You do not need to set it for this exercise.) You can also change the color of the hotspot using the color box in the Property inspector.

The Alt text appears in the browser when the user rolls over the hotspot area. Adding some descriptive text helps users determine whether they want to link to that page. This feature may not be supported in earlier browsers, but it is a good idea to add Alt text to all of your links.

6) For this exercise, add some descriptive text in the Alt text box for each hotspot. For example, type *Sweet Creations Home* for the Web address, *Internet Special* for the candy stick, and *Sweet Deals* for the candy.

TIP *You can change the shape of the hotspot using the Shape pop-up menu in the Property inspector. If you change the shape, you may need to resize or move the hotspot to cover the area.*

7) Choose File > Save As and save the banner.png file in the Lesson07 folder.

In Lesson 8, you will export this file as a GIF image.

WORKING WITH THE WEB LAYER

Hotspots and slices (covered later in this lesson) are stored on the Web Layer on the Layers panel. The Web Layer is the top layer by default and cannot be moved. As you work with your images, you may want to hide the hotspots or slices to edit the objects below. You can click Show/Hide Slices on the Tools panel or use the Layers panel. If you use the Tools panel, all hotspots, slices, and slice guides are hidden. If you use the Layers panel, you can hide individual slices or hotspots.

1) Choose Window > Layers to open the Layers panel.

The Layers panel displays the Web Layer as the top layer.

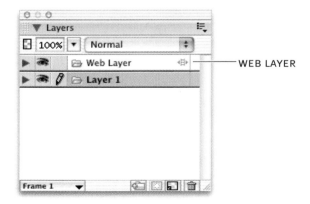

WEB LAYER

2) Click the plus (Windows) or triangle (Macintosh) to expand the Web Layer.

The three hotspots for the image map are displayed as separate objects on the Layers panel.

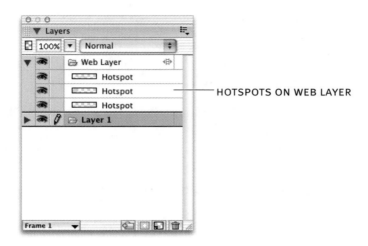

HOTSPOTS ON WEB LAYER

3) Click the Hide Layer icon (the eye) on one of the hotspot objects.

The hotspot on the canvas is hidden. Click the Show/Hide Layer icon again to view the hotspot.

TIP *If you hide the Web Layer on the Layers panel, hotspots will still be exported when you export as HTML.*

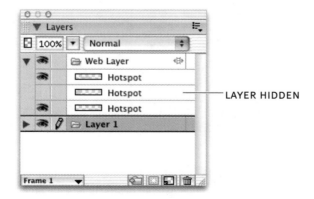

LAYER HIDDEN

NOTE *You can click the lock column (the column with the pencil) on the Web Layer to ensure that you don't delete or move the hotspots or slices. For this exercise, leave the Web Layer unlocked.*

SLICING AN IMAGE

The final goal of all your work on the home page you've been creating is to export the page as HTML, which you will do in Lesson 8. Your page currently consists of four buttons and several graphic elements—the logo, some text, a picture, and so on. If you exported the page now, you would get several large images along with the buttons. To see what that means, look at your home page. Click Show Slices and Hotspots on the Tools panel if you don't see the slices on the buttons. If you don't see the slice guides for your buttons, choose View > Slice Guides.

The red guides indicate the areas that will be sliced—or cut—when you export the page. Imagine using a ruler and a knife and cutting the canvas using the red lines as your guides. The resulting pieces would be the images you would get when you exported the page. Some of the images are large and could take longer to download. What you want to do is to create smaller slices that logically divide your page.

When you slice the canvas, not only are you dividing the image into smaller pieces, you are also defining the HTML table that will be created. An HTML table is a series of rows and columns in which you can place text or graphics. Tables are the best way to control the look of your page. The rows and columns in the table can be of any height and width, and you can have columns or rows that expand over other columns or rows on the page.

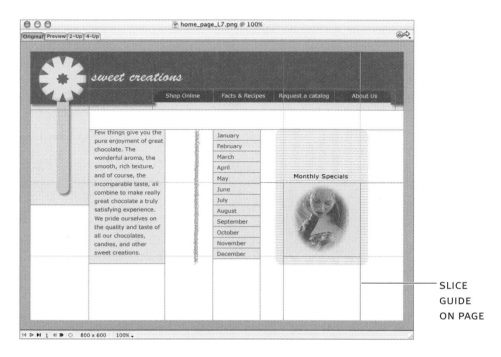

SLICE GUIDE ON PAGE

There are several advantages to slicing an image. For example, if you will be updating a section of a graphic often, if you use slicing you will have to redo just that one piece of the graphic. In addition, each slice can be optimized differently for better overall results: for part of the image, JPEG may be the best choice for exporting, and for another part, GIF may be the best choice.

Slicing also is a way to add some interactivity to the page. The slices on your buttons were added automatically for you when you used the Button Editor. You could have added the rollovers manually—though why would you want to when they are so easy to create in the Button Editor? However, there are other interactive elements such as disjointed rollovers and pop-up menus that you can add. You will create disjointed rollovers in this lesson and add pop-up menus in Lesson 10.

ADDING A SLICE

You can add a slice to the page in several ways. You can use the Slice tool and draw the slice, or you can select an object and have Fireworks create the slice for you based on the size and placement of the selected object.

1) Open your home_page.png file from Lesson 7 if it is not already open.

You can use the home_page_L7.png in the Start folder within the Lesson07 folder if you no longer have your file. Use Save As and remove the L7 from the name and then save the new file in the Lesson07 folder.

2) Select the white square on the Specials layer.

The image of the girl is on top of the square. Make sure that you select the square, not the girl.

3) Choose Edit > Insert > Slice.

A slice is created on the object. If you want the slice to be the same size as the object, this is the quickest method.

4) Select the Slice tool on the Tools panel and then draw a rectangle over the text block on the left of the canvas.

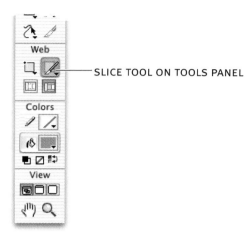

SLICE TOOL ON TOOLS PANEL

You can adjust or move the slice with the Pointer tool once it is created. Drag any of the corner handles to change the size. Use the red slice guides to help you as you add slices to the page. Remember that the red guides are defining the HTML table for the page.

5) Draw another slice on the January text.

Each month will have a separate slice, and you want them all the same size. Make sure that this slice is wide enough for all of the other months to fit, too.

TIP *Since the September text is the longest, you could draw the slice on this text first and then move it over the January text.*

173

6) Switch to the Pointer tool and then hold down Alt (Windows) or Option (Macintosh) as you drag the slice to make a copy of it. Add Shift as you drag to constrain the movement to a vertical line. Choose Edit > Repeat Duplicate to create slices for the remaining months.

You learned this method for creating multiple copies of an element in Lesson 5. For this example, the slices need to cover the text. You may need to move your slices if they are in the wrong positions.

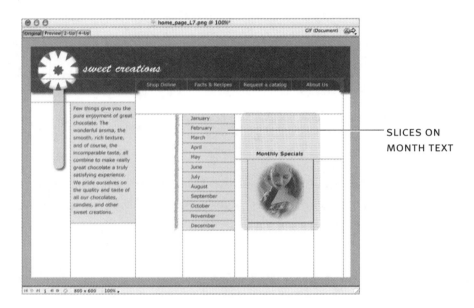

SLICES ON
MONTH TEXT

TIP *If you have Snap to Guides turned on, your slices snap to the nearest guide as you move them. Turn off Snap to Guides to make moving the slices easier.*

CREATING DISJOINTED ROLLOVERS

In Lesson 6, you learned to use the Button Editor to create rollovers in which one image is swapped out for another image when the user moves over it. A disjointed rollover is an image that changes when the user moves the pointer over a completely different image.

On your home page, you want to display your monthly specials. As the user rolls over a month name, you want a new image to appear within the white square.

Disjointed rollovers use frames to store the rollover images. In this lesson, you learn how to add the frames and import the rollover images.

ADDING FRAMES

Frames are places to store the various states of your rollovers. When you used the Button Editor, Fireworks placed the Over state of the button in Frame 2 and the Down state in Frame 3. This was all done automatically for you. For the disjointed rollovers you are creating in this exercise, you add frames and place the images individually.

1) Choose Window > Frames to open the Frames panel.

The Frames panel is in the Frames and History panel group. You could also click the disclosure triangle to view the panel.

2) Select Add Frames from the Frames Option menu. Type *12* in the Number text box, select After Current Frame, and then click OK.

You want a different image for each month of the year, plus the original image (the girl), for a total of 13 frames.

3) Click Hide Slices and Hotspots on the Tools panel; then select Frame 2 and then Frame 3 on the Frames panel.

In Frame 2, you see the Over state of your buttons; in Frame 3, you see the Down state of your buttons. The Button Editor placed these images in these frames for you.

TIP *Hiding the slices makes it easier to see the buttons in the different frames. When you roll over Show or Hide Slices and Hotspots on the Tools panel, the tooltip tells you the shortcut (the number 2) for showing and hiding the guides. As you work with slices, you may find it faster to press 2 to show and hide them than to use the Tools panel.*

4) Select Frame 1 and then select the white square.

Look at the Property inspector to see the X and Y values for the square. You are going to place new images in each of the new frames you just added. Each image must be the same size and in the same position as the square.

You could remember the X and Y values and then use those numbers as you place the new images. It would be easier to draw some ruler guides and use those for placing the images. Guides you draw on Frame 1 appear on all of the frames.

5) Drag ruler guides to the top, left, bottom, and right of the square.

You will place all of the new images within the center of those guides.

6) Select Frame 2. Import the january.png file from the Months folder in the Lesson07 folder. Place the image (a cup of hot chocolate) within the ruler guides.

All of the images you need for each month are in this folder. In Lesson 1, you created the images for December and September. If you no longer have those files, you can use the ones in the Months folder in the Lesson07 folder.

JANUARY IMAGE WITHIN RULER GUIDES

7) Select the remaining frames and place the remaining images.

Frame 1 has the start image, Frame 2 has the January image, Frame 3 has the February image, and so on.

8) For the next steps, you need to see the slices, so click Show Slices again on the Tools panel and select Frame 1.

Don't forget: you can also use the shortcut to show the slices—press 2 to toggle the slice guides.

ADDING A BEHAVIOR

In these next steps, you will identify the frame that is associated with each month. The process is as easy as dragging from one slice and dropping onto another.

1) Select the slice for January.

The center marker (the behavior handle) makes it easy to add the interactivity to this button. If you are familiar with Dreamweaver, you'll recognize the icon that appears when you click the slice. In Fireworks, you use this handle to point to the slice over the image you want to swap out when the user rolls over the button.

2) Drag the behavior handle from the January slice to the slice on the image to create the disjointed rollover.

You'll see a blue line connecting the two slices, and the Swap Image dialog box will appear.

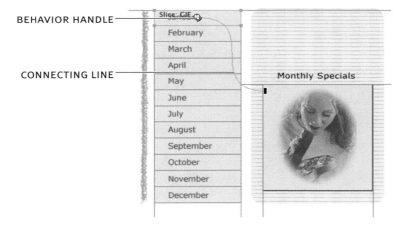

3) In the Swap Image dialog box, choose the frame that stores the rollover image. For this exercise, the January image is drawn in Frame 2, so choose Frame 2. Click OK.

4) Repeat steps 1 through 3 for the slices on the remaining months.

As you drag the behavior handles on the slices to the image slice, remember that Frame 1 contains the starting image. The month number (1 through 12) corresponds to the frame number plus one. Therefore, January goes in Frame 2, February goes in Frame 3, and so on.

5) Save your file; then click the Preview tab to see your rollovers.

Roll over each month and see if the starting image changes to a new image. When you roll over another month, the image swaps to that month's image. When you roll off the months, the image returns to the starting image.

If you have the same image in two months, then you chose the same frame in the Swap Image dialog box. Click the Original tab and redo those months. Just drag the behavior handles as you did originally and choose a new frame number.

NOTE *When you are previewing your page, you might notice that areas without slices don't appear on the canvas. They aren't missing. Your document hasn't been set to display areas without slices. In the next lesson, you will learn the settings for exporting as HTML. For now, if you want to see the entire page, choose File > HTML Setup and then click the Document Specific tab. Choose Include Areas without Slices. If you are still in preview mode, your page updates, and the remaining areas appear. This option is normally selected by default.*

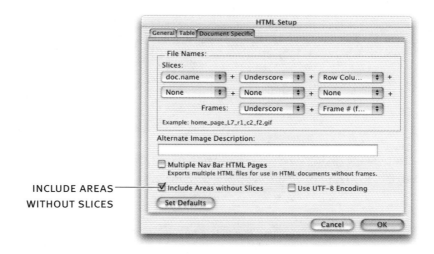

INCLUDE AREAS WITHOUT SLICES

VIEWING FULL SCREEN

When viewing your page on the Preview tab, you see the menu bar and all of the panels. You can easily hide the panels and the menus to get an uncluttered view of your page.

1) Click the Full-Screen Mode button on the Tools panel.

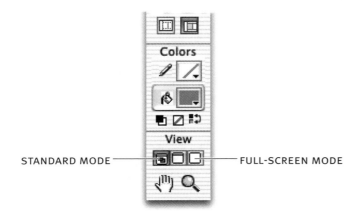

STANDARD MODE ———— FULL-SCREEN MODE

Your page is centered on the screen with a black background. If you click the center button, your page is centered on the screen, but you still see the menus.

POWER TIP *You can also use the shortcut key—the F key—to toggle through the screen modes. Press the F key twice to switch to full-screen mode; press it once to switch to full-screen mode with menus.*

2) Press Tab to hide the panels.

Your page is displayed without menus or any of the panels.

3) Press Tab again to display the panels and then click the Standard Screen Mode button.

Full-screen mode is helpful when you want an uncluttered view of your page, but you'll need the menus back to continue working on your document.

ADDING MORE SLICES

You added slices on the buttons and the rollovers to control the interactivity of those areas. You can also add slices to create links for graphics or to control the cells of the table that is created when you export the page. You will use the top portion of this page—the logo, the buttons, and the red header section—on the other pages of your site. The candy in the logo would be a good place to add a link that returns the user to this home page. To add the link, you need to add a slice.

1) Select the Slice tool and draw a slice on the candy. Draw another slice on the candy stick.

Remember that the slices are defining cells in the HTML table. Make sure that the widths of these two slices are the same. Adjust each slice if necessary to make them the same. Use the red slice guides to help position or size the slices.

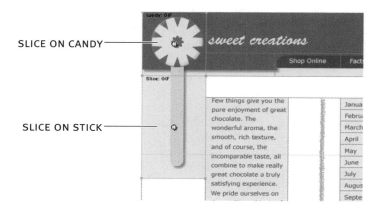

NOTE *You may need to move the text block if it is too close to the stick.*

2) Select the slice over the candy. In the Property inspector, type *candy* in the Slice Name text box. In the Link text box, type *home_page.htm*. In the Alt text box type *Return Home*.

Your entry in the Name text box is used as the name of the graphic when you export your page. Your entry in the Link text box is the name of the HTML file for your home page.

3) Select the slice over the candy stick. In the Property inspector, type *stick* in the Slice Name text box. Add a slice to the text block and to each of the remaining areas of the red header.

Use the red slice guides to help you determine areas that need smaller slices.

NOTE *You will use the top header portion of this page, along with the buttons, the candy logo, and the stick, on the remaining pages that you build. By adding the slices and naming the slices, you ensure that all of the other pages use the same images for the top portion of the HTML page.*

4) Save your file.

You will use this file in the next lesson.

ON YOUR OWN

Did you notice that the starting image in Frame 1 has a thin black border around it? That is the border on the white square. If you like that border, you can copy the square and then paste it in Frame 2. The square is pasted in the proper place but has a solid fill. Remove the fill and then copy the square and paste in the remaining frames. If you don't like the border, then just remove it from Frame 1.

Finally—your page is complete. Don't take that coffee break yet. In the next lesson, you will set the optimization for each of the slices and then export the page as HTML.

WHAT YOU HAVE LEARNED

In this lesson, you have:

- Added hotspots to a graphic and added links for an image map [pages 166–169]
- Examined the Web Layer [pages 169–170]
- Added slices to an image [pages 171–174]
- Added frames to your document and placed images in the frames [pages 175–176]
- Created disjointed rollovers [pages 177–178]
- Viewed your page in full-screen mode [page 179]

optimizing and exporting

After you complete your artwork, you need to export it. Whether you want to use your images on the Web or for multimedia presentations, Fireworks provides several methods for creating the best-quality images with the smallest-possible file sizes. Fireworks exports the following formats: GIF, JPEG, PNG, TIFF, PICT (Macintosh), BMP, PSD, Flash SWF, Illustrator 7, Lotus Domino Designer, and WBMP. WBMP (Wireless Bitmap) is the graphic format optimized for mobile computing devices.

Exporting your images is actually a two-step process. First, you set the optimizing parameters you want for your image on the Optimize panel; then you export the image, saving it according to your optimization settings.

Fireworks's native file format is PNG. Although it is possible to use a PNG file in a Web page, this is not the best option. You should always keep a copy of your original PNG files along with the exported files you create. The PNG format retains your editable text, effects, and vector objects, so you can easily make changes. If you need to change an image, change the PNG file and then re-export it to get the graphic you place on your Web page.

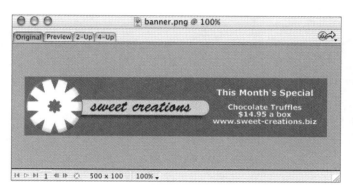

Creating small, high-quality images is one of Firework's strengths. In this lesson you will learn the proper way to optimize, and then export your graphics for good-looking images on your Web pages.

WHAT YOU WILL LEARN

In this lesson, you will:

• Examine the various color palettes available in Fireworks

• Use the Export wizard

• Set the target export file size

• Use the Optimize panel

• Save export settings

APPROXIMATE TIME

This lesson takes approximately 1 hour to complete.

LESSON FILES

Media Files:

Lesson08\about.htm

Lesson08\facts.htm

Lesson08\request.htm

Lesson08\shop.htm

Starting Files:

Lesson08\Start\banner.png

Lesson08\Start\home_page_L8.png

Completed Projects:

Lesson08\Completed\banner.png

Lesson08\Completed\banner.gif

USING THE EXPORT WIZARD

The Export wizard provides a quick way to export your files. The wizard asks a series of questions and then suggests file types and optimization settings. You can also set a file size for the Export wizard to use as a target for the optimization. At the end of the question dialog boxes, the Export Preview dialog box opens with the optimization suggestions.

Ad banners are sprinkled throughout the Web. If you buy ad space on a Web site to place a banner, you are usually given a width and height size for your ad, along with a file size limit. The Export wizard is great for optimizing your ads; you just enter the maximum file size, and the wizard does the rest.

1) Open the banner.png file you created in Lesson 7.

If you no longer have that file, you can use the banner.png file in the Start folder within the Lesson08 folder.

2) Choose File > Export Wizard. Select the Target Export File Size option and type *15* in the text box; then click Continue.

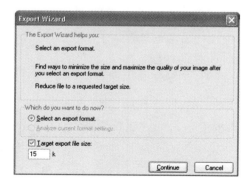

If you select Target Export File Size in the Export wizard, Fireworks attempts to optimize the file at that size by adjusting the quality of JPEG files, modifying the smoothing for JPEG files, changing the number of colors for GIF files, and changing dithering settings for GIF files. This feature is especially important when you want to create images or animated GIF files that don't exceed maximum file size limits for banner ads on commercial sites.

3) In the Choose Destination dialog box (also named Export Wizard), select The web; then click Continue.

Your destination choice determines the file type for exporting your file. Selecting the web or Dreamweaver results in a GIF or JPEG image. Selecting an image editing application or a desktop publishing application results in a TIFF image. After several seconds, the Analysis Results screen displays Fireworks's recommendations.

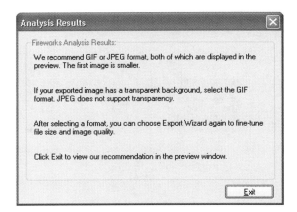

4) Click Exit to go to the Export Preview window.

The top right preview displays the image as a GIF file; the bottom right preview displays the image in JPEG format. Here you can use the settings Fireworks chose or make adjustments on your own.

5) Click the top right preview and then the bottom right preview to display the settings the wizard chose for you.

Each preview displays the export format, the number of colors, the file size, and the estimated time needed to download the image. The download time is based on a 56-Kbps download speed. The speed option cannot be changed.

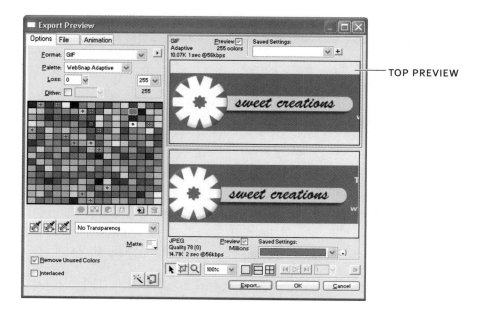

6) Click the preview you want to use and then click Export to export the image.

When choosing the export format, you need to look at the quality of the image within the preview window along with the file size. In this exercise, the GIF and JPEG images both look the same. The JPEG file size is 14.7K, whereas the GIF file size is 10K. Your choice here would be the GIF image.

TIP *To see other portions of the image, drag the image within the preview. When you drag within the preview, the pointer turns to the hand pointer.*

7) In the Save As Type (Windows) or Save As (Macintosh) pop-up menu, choose Images Only, change Slices to None, and navigate to the Lesson08 folder. Click Save to export and save your file.

NOTE *The hotspots you added to the image in Lesson 7 will not be exported when you export the image. Later in this lesson, you will learn to export both the HTML and the image.*

ON YOUR OWN

Use the same file (banner.png) and repeat the Export Wizard command. This time, enter 8 for the target file size. Look at the difference between the GIF and JPEG images. The quality of the JPEG image diminishes at this lower file size. You don't need to export this file again.

CHOOSING THE IMAGE FORMAT

The Export wizard does a good job of analyzing banner ads for you, but normally you will want to take control over the image optimization and export settings.

Picking the correct image format is crucial to the optimization process. The most popular file formats for Web graphics are GIF and JPEG. GIF images are generally used for line art and images with solid colors. GIF images can contain transparent areas and can be used for animation files. The disadvantage of GIF images is that they are restricted to 256 colors. JPEG is generally used for photographic images or images with gradients and more colors. JPEG files cannot be transparent or used in animations.

You use the Optimize panel to pick the formatting options for exporting the file or for each slice. To take more control over the optimization process, you will want to set the optimization for each slice.

1) Open the home_page.png file in Lesson 7 that you've been working on.

You can open the home_page_L8.png file in the Lesson08 Start folder if you no longer have your file; then rename that file home_page.png.

2) Choose Window > Optimize to access the Optimize panel. Choose GIF from the Export File Format pop-up menu.

You can also click the disclosure triangle to open the panel if it is docked in the panel group.

If you choose GIF as your export file format, you need to pick the color palette for the export. GIF files can be up to 256 colors (actually, only 216 colors; the other 40 colors are used by the operating system and the browser).

3) Choose Adaptive from the Indexed Palette pop-up menu. Change the number of colors to 256 in the Colors pop-up menu.

The color palette is a group of colors used in the image. Fireworks contains 10 preset palettes for you to use.

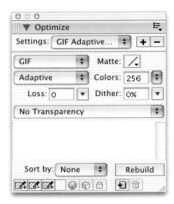

The following list describes the default palettes.

- **Adaptive**: Creates a custom palette containing the majority of the colors in the image, whether or not they are Web-safe colors.

- **WebSnap Adaptive (Windows) or Web Adaptive (Macintosh)**: Creates a bridge between the Web 216 palette and the Adaptive palette. Colors within a tolerance range of seven color spaces are snapped to the closest Web-safe color.

- **Web 216**: Displays a palette of 216 colors that have a similar appearance on both Windows and Macintosh computers. This is sometimes referred to as a Web-safe or browser-safe palette because it generates the most similar results on different platforms and different browsers. Each color in the image is replaced with the closest Web-safe color.

- **Exact**: Contains the exact colors in the image when the image contains 256 colors or less. If the image contains more than 256 colors, the WebSnap Adaptive palette is used as the default.

- **Macintosh**: Contains 256 colors as defined by the Macintosh system colors.

- **Windows**: Contains 256 colors as defined by the Windows system colors.

- **Grayscale**: Displays a palette of 256 (or fewer) shades of gray. Using this palette converts your image to grayscale.

- **Black & White**: Displays a palette of only two colors: black and white.

- **Uniform**: Displays a mathematical palette based on RGB pixel values.

- **Custom**: Gives the user the option of importing another color palette saved from Fireworks or Adobe Photoshop.

USING THE 4-UP PREVIEW TAB

Fireworks enables you to preview your images within the document window before exporting them. You can determine the export settings on the page as you create it and preview the results. You can also split the document window into two or four preview areas to view different settings. Fireworks also displays the file size and the approximate download times within each preview.

1) Click the 4-Up tab at the top of the document window.

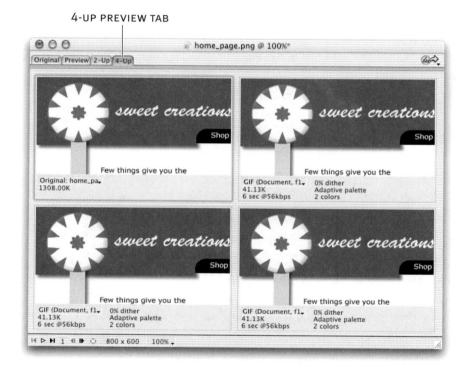

4-UP PREVIEW TAB

While previewing, you cannot make any changes to the image. The 2-Up tab divides the document into two previews; the 4-Up tab divides the document into four previews. In 2-Up and 4-Up modes, the upper left preview displays the original image and can be edited. The other areas are previews only.

TIP *You can display the original image (or no original image) in any of the preview areas in 2-Up and 4-Up preview modes. Select Original from the pop-up menu at the bottom of the preview area.*

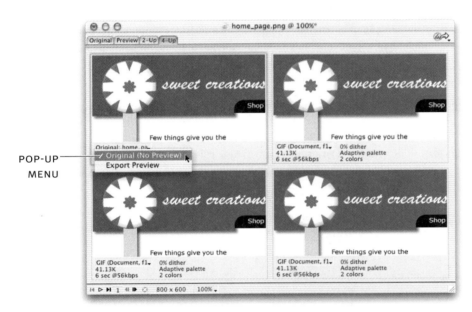

POP-UP
MENU

2) Click anywhere within the bottom right preview to select this window.

A black border (blue in Macintosh OS X) appears around the selected preview. The selected preview reflects any changes you make on the Optimize panel.

TIP *When you were in the Export Preview window, the pointer turned to the hand pointer when you dragged within the panel. In the preview area, you need to select the Hand tool from the Tools panel to move the image within the preview. You can also hold down the Spacebar as you drag within the panel to switch to the Hand tool automatically. That shortcut also works when you are editing in the document window.*

3) On the Optimize panel, change the Index Palette to Web 216 and set the number of colors to 32 for the color palette in the Colors pop-up menu.

Choosing a smaller number reduces the file size. Look at the top right panel and compare the file size and the number of colors. Depending on your image, your file size may be reduced significantly. With this page, you should see a significant change. Use the Hand tool, or hold down the Spacebar as you drag around in the preview window to see the image of the girl, and look at the graininess of her image.

Also look at the quality of the image after you reduce the number of colors. If you pick a number that is smaller than the actual number of colors in the image, some colors are lost. The pixels with the lost colors are converted to the closest remaining colors on the palette.

4) Reduce the Dither amount by dragging the slider on the Optimize panel to zero.

Dithering is a process of approximating colors not on the current palette. A dithered image often looks "noisy," or grainy; however, dithering can help smooth out the banding created by a gradient-like transition of colors. The higher the number, the more dithering that occurs and the larger the file size.

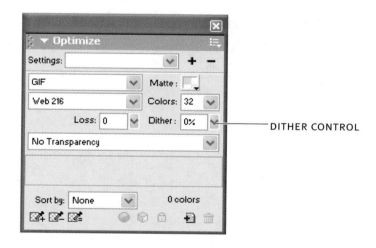

DITHER CONTROL

Look at the file size now that the dithering is removed. There is a noticeable difference in the file size, but the quality of the image has suffered and is unacceptable.

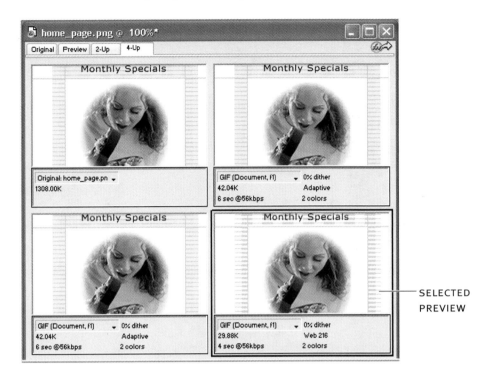

Using each of the four previews, you can see the results of the changes you make to the optimization settings. Once you are satisfied with your settings, click within the preview you want to use to select it.

5) Click the Original tab to return to the document window.

The settings you chose for the selected preview are now applied to the document and will be used when you export the file.

USING PRESET OPTIMIZATION SETTINGS

There are several preset settings you can also use to quickly set the file format for your images. Once you pick one of the presets, you can always modify them for further control over your images.

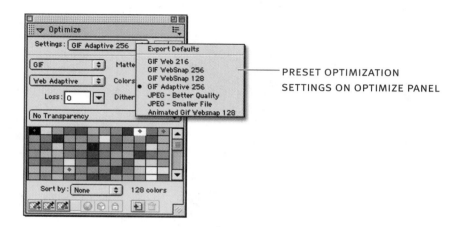

PRESET OPTIMIZATION
SETTINGS ON OPTIMIZE PANEL

The presets are listed in the Settings pop-up menu on the Optimize panel. If you have a slice selected, the Property inspector displays a Slice Export Setting pop-up menu from which you can choose from one of the optimization settings.

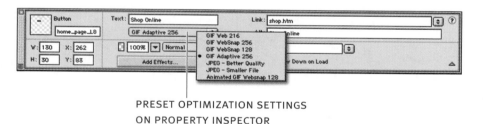

PRESET OPTIMIZATION SETTINGS
ON PROPERTY INSPECTOR

EXPORTING JPEG IMAGES

The GIF option exports 8-bit images, or a maximum of 256 colors, and works well for line art and images with solid colors. For photographs or any artwork with gradations or millions of colors, you'll want to export in JPEG format. JPEG is a lossy compression scheme, meaning that it looks at your image and removes information as part of its compression algorithm.

On the home page you are creating, you have some buttons, some text, the logo, and the images used for the disjointed rollovers. The GIF controls you set in the last exercise will work for all areas of the page except for the images in the disjointed rollovers. For these images, you want to use JPEG compression. You already have a slice over the exact area that you used to create the rollovers. You can simply select the slice and change the optimization settings for just that slice.

1) Select the slice over the picture of the girl. Select JPEG from the Export File Format pop-up menu on the Optimize panel. Click the 4-Up tab to preview the image. Use the Hand tool to move the girl into view.

By increasing the compression level in a JPEG image, you reduce the quality. In this image, the quality is set to 80 percent.

2) Select the image in the top right preview and then drag the Quality slider on the Optimize panel to 60 percent.

Look at the image compared to those in the other preview windows. It appears softer, but still is an acceptable image. The file size is a little smaller.

3) Select the image in the bottom right preview and drag the Quality slider on the Optimize panel to 35 percent.

At this setting, the image displays compression artifacts—areas where you can see blocks of pixels. The file size savings does not justify the quality loss.

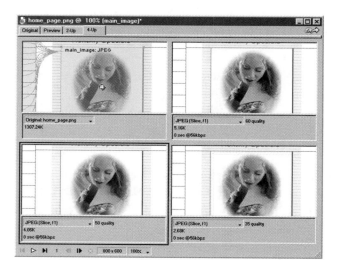

4) Select the image in the bottom left preview. Move the Quality slider to 50 percent and change smoothing to 1 in the Smoothing pop-up menu.

The compression scheme in JPEG format sometimes leaves rough or blocky areas on the image. Smoothing is a method of blurring those rough edges so they are not as noticeable. The file size is reduced slightly with smoothing.

After you choose your export file format settings, you can save them for future export operations or for batch processing. All of the settings on the Optimize panel are saved.

196

5) Select the top right preview.

You want to save the optimization settings used on this preview. These settings are used when you export or save the settings or save the file.

6) Click the plus button to the right of the Settings pop-up menu. Type a name for your settings in the Preset Name text box. Click OK.

The name of the saved settings now appears in the Settings pop-up list on the Optimize panel. This collection of settings remains for your use until you delete it. To use these settings in other images, choose the name of the settings from the Settings pop-up menu on the Optimize panel.

7) Click the Original tab to return to the document window and save your file.

Your settings are available for you to use on all your images where you want the same optimize options. To use your saved settings, choose the name from the Settings pop-up menu on the Optimize panel.

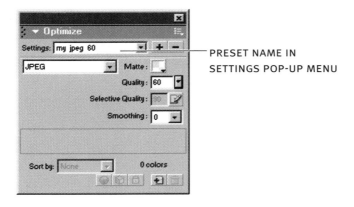

PRESET NAME IN
SETTINGS POP-UP MENU

PREVIEWING IN THE BROWSER

The Preview tab in the document window provides a good method for viewing your page. You can also preview the page in a browser before you export it, to make sure it is to your liking.

1) Choose File > Preview in Browser.

If a primary browser has been set up, you will see it listed in the submenu. You can then select the browser from the submenu.

2) If you do not see a browser in the list, choose Set Primary Browser from the submenu. In the Locate Browser dialog box, navigate to the location of the browser application you want to use as your main browser. Select the browser and then click Open.

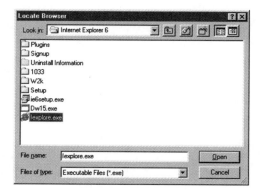

After you set your browser, repeat step 1. If you want to set a secondary browser, repeat step 2, choosing Set Secondary Browser from the submenu.

Your page opens in the browser.

EXPORTING AS HTML

You are now ready to export your document and create the HTML page that displays the page with your buttons and rollovers. Fireworks does all the work; you just have to set up the location where you want all your files saved.

1) Choose File > Export. Navigate to the Lesson08 folder. In the Save As Type (Windows) or Save As (Macintosh) pop-up menu, select HTML and Images. From the HTML pop-up menu, select Export HTML File.

For this page, you want not only the images with the HTML code for the rollovers; you also want the page exported as HTML. You also want to make sure that you select the Lesson08 folder for exporting your files. That folder includes some HTML documents for testing the links on your buttons.

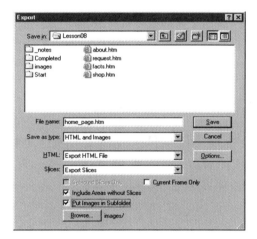

2) Select Export Slices from the Slices pop-up menu.

The slice (the translucent green area on top of each button) determines how Fireworks creates (cuts) the buttons. If you don't export the slices, the page is exported as one image. The slice also enables the JavaScript for rollovers—if slices are not exported, your rollovers will not work.

NOTE *Select Include Areas without Slices to create a graphic for areas without a slice. If you deselect this option, you create empty cells in the HTML table.*

3) Select Put Images in Subfolder.

Generally, you will want to separate your images from the HTML files. This is a file maintenance and organization issue only, but highly recommended. Fireworks defaults to a subfolder named Images. When you select Put Images in Subfolder, you'll see the default folder name—Images—next to the Browse button. If you want to store your images in a folder other than the Images folder, click the Browse button and locate the folder.

There is an Images folder already created in the Lesson08 folder for you to store your images. You don't need to click the Browse button for this exercise. If the folder did not exist, Fireworks would create one for you.

The files you export from Fireworks need to be saved in a folder (or in subfolder) that is defined (or will be defined) as a site in Dreamweaver. In Lesson 11, you will define the Lessons folder as the local site folder.

NOTE *Some folder names and file names are capitalized in this book for readability. Some Web servers do not support capital letters for file names. When you are building your images and HTML pages, it is a good idea to use lowercase for all of your file names. That way, you can be sure that the file names are supported on any server.*

4) Click Options to define the HTML options that Fireworks uses when generating the HTML.

You need to set several options to define how Fireworks creates the HTML file. These options are defined in the HTML Setup dialog box. You can access this dialog box from the Export dialog box, as you just did, or you can choose File > HTML Setup.

On the General tab of the HTML Setup dialog box, you can choose the HTML style that Fireworks generates and the file extension.

5) For this exercise, with the General tab selected, choose Dreamweaver HTML from the pop-up menu. Select htm (.htm) as the extension. If you are using a Macintosh, choose Dreamweaver from the File Creator pop-up menu.

The method Fireworks uses to create the HTML depends on the HTML style you choose from the pop-up menu. Fireworks supports Dreamweaver, FrontPage, GoLive, and a generic style. Since you will be using Dreamweaver in Lesson 11, you want Fireworks to generate the proper code for Dreamweaver when it exports the HTML.

On the Extension pop-up menu, you can choose from a variety of popular extensions. If the one you need doesn't appear in the list, you can enter the extension in the text box.

The Include HTML Comments check box determines whether Fireworks inserts comments in the HTML code. Comments show where you should copy the code if you are pasting the code in an HTML editor. If you are familiar with HTML, you might not need the comments, so deselect this option to cut down on the code that Fireworks produces. In Lesson 11, you will use Dreamweaver to examine the HTML files, so you don't need to select this option.

The Lowercase File Name check box forces Fireworks to generate all-lowercase file names when it exports your files. Since many Web servers are case sensitive, it is a good idea to use lowercase for all of your file names. That way, there is no confusion, and your naming convention is consistent.

The File Creator option for the Macintosh enables you to double-click the file to open Dreamweaver from the Finder.

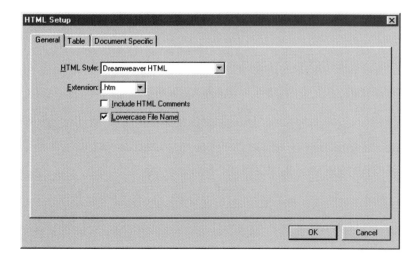

6) Select the Table tab.

The Table tab allows you to modify the spacing in the table that Fireworks creates. For this exercise, you will use all of the defaults.

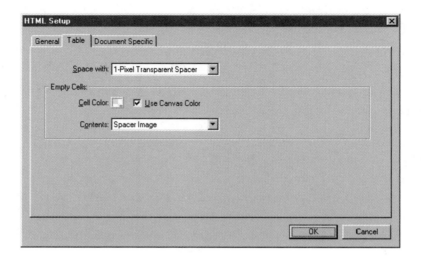

Whenever you have slices on your page, Fireworks generates an HTML table when it generates the HTML file. In the Space With pop-up menu, you can choose from 1-Pixel Transparent Spacer (the default), Nested Tables - No Spacers, or Single Table – No Spacers. If you choose the 1-Pixel – No Spacer option, Fireworks inserts a transparent GIF image. If you choose the Nested Tables option, Fireworks creates tables within tables to replicate the page. This creates complicated code, but it is fairly accurate. If you choose the Single Table option, the code is minimal, but the page may not appear correctly in all browsers.

If the table has empty cells, you can set the method that Fireworks uses to fill the cells: None, Spacer Image, or Non-breaking Space. You choose these methods from the Contents pop-up menu. Choosing None is not recommended as browsers may not render the table properly when the cells are empty. Choosing Spacer Image (the default) inserts a transparent GIF image in the cell. Fireworks creates a small image named spacer.gif and uses that image in all of the tables it generates. Choosing Non-breaking Space inserts the code for a space ( ) in the cell.

7) Select the Document Specific tab. Set the first row of slices to doc.name + Underscore + Row Column..., and set Frames to Underscore + Frame#.

On the Document Specific tab, you can customize the file naming scheme for the images in the rollovers. As you choose from each of the pop-up menus, an example of the resulting file name appears. For this example, you use doc.name + Underscore + Frame #. Set the other options to None.

The resulting file name appears as home_page_f2.gif in the dialog box.

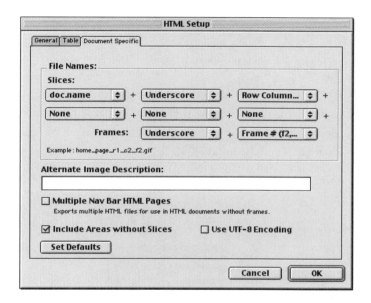

Select Include Areas without Slices to ensure that the entire document is exported. If this option is not selected, areas without slices do not appear when you view your document in the preview window, and they are not exported.

You can enter an alternate image description in this dialog box that is applied to each image in the table. As you learned in Lesson 6, the Alt text enhances your site's accessibility. Although you can enter a universal value here, you should add Alt text to each slice instead.

NOTE *There are several options for naming your rollover file names. You could also choose Rollover from the Frames pop-up menu to add _over instead of _f2 at the end of the file name.*

TIP *If you find yourself setting the options in this dialog box over and over and you consistently use the same settings, click Set Defaults to retain your current settings.*

8) Click OK to close the HTML Setup dialog box and then click Save to export your slices and create the HTML page.

Fireworks exports your images using the Optimization settings on the Optimize panel and creates an HTML file.

9) Open the HTML file in your browser to check the results.

The buttons and the links should work.

10) Save and close your file.

USING THE QUICK EXPORT BUTTON

The Quick Export button, located at the top right of the document window, is a shortcut menu for exporting your files to other Macromedia applications such as Dreamweaver, Macromedia Flash, FreeHand, and Director as well as applications such as Adobe Photoshop and Adobe GoLive.

You can also use the Quick Export button to launch your browser or other Macromedia application.

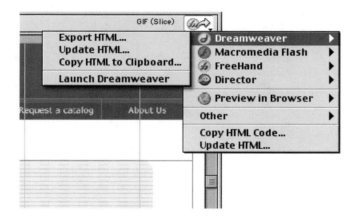

WHAT YOU HAVE LEARNED

In this lesson, you have:

- Used the Export Wizard to optimize a banner ad [pages 184–187]

- Used the Optimize panel to pick the image export format [pages 187–189]

- Used the 4-Up tab to preview export settings [pages 190–193]

- Examined the preset optimization settings [page 194]

- Changed the optimization for a slice to JPEG [pages 195–197]

- Defined a preview browser [page 198]

- Exported the page as HTML [pages 199–204]

- Examined the Quick Export button [page 204]

creating gif animations

LESSON 9

Animated GIF images use a variant of CompuServe's Graphics Interchange Format. In 1987, the specification was enhanced to enable GIF files to contain multiple images that play sequentially to provide flip-book-style animation. A 1989 amendment to the format added such controls as an optional delay between frames.

For all their advantages, animated GIF images aren't perfect. Because they are GIF files, they're limited to 256 colors. GIF files are far from ideal for photographic images, such as a time-lapse view of a sunset. They're best for animated banners, buttons, and line art.

You can stop a looping GIF animation with a browser's Stop button and start over by reloading the image, but you can't stop and resume playback where you left off. If you need VCR-like playback control, use a commercial animation program such as Macromedia Flash or Director.

Animated GIF images are silent movies; if you want to mix sound and animation, use Apple QuickTime movies or Macromedia Flash.

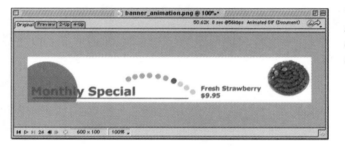

This image displays several frames of the animation you will create in this lesson.

Despite its shortcomings, the animated GIF file is a good medium for simple Web animation—no plug-ins, no server tweaking, and relatively mild browser-compatibility headaches. GIF animation is a simple technology that came to lead the field because it's simple. In a Web world increasingly obsessed with bells and whistles, that's an important lesson.

WHAT YOU WILL LEARN

In this lesson, you will:

- Create GIF animations

- Use onion skinning

- Change the playback settings for an animated GIF image

- Use tweening to rotate an item

- Create symbols and use the symbol library

- Use an animation symbol

APPROXIMATE TIME

This lesson takes approximately 1 hour to complete.

LESSON FILES

Media Files:
Lesson09\Media\strawberry_pie.png

Starting Files:
None

Completed Projects:
Lesson09\Completed\banner_animation.png

CREATING AN ANIMATION

This exercise demonstrates basic frame-by-frame animation for creating an animated GIF image. You'll draw a shape and move it across the page. If you want to see the final animation, open the banner_animation.png file in the Completed folder within the Lesson09 folder.

1) Create a new document. Make the canvas size 600 by 100 pixels and the color white. Save your file in the Lesson09 folder and name it banner_animation.png.

2) Draw a circle on the canvas. Change the fill color of the circle to the red color you used for the candy logo and remove the stroke.

Make the circle the same size as the height of the canvas; 100 pixels.

3) In the Property inspector, change the opacity of the circle to 50 percent.

The circle should now be a pink color.

4) Move the circle to the bottom left corner of the canvas, partially off the canvas.

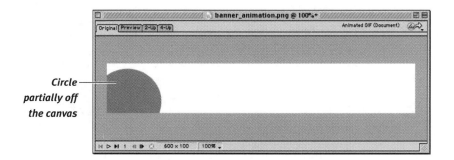

Circle partially off the canvas

5) Select the Text tool, type *Monthly Special*, and then use the Line tool to draw a line under the text. Rename the layer *Special*.

Change the font for the text to Verdana bold, 25 points and change the color to the same red you used for the circle. Move the text to the bottom left of the canvas.

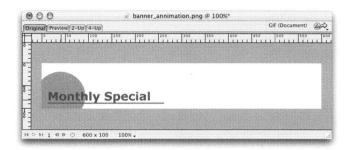

6) Create a new layer and name it *Animation*.

Make sure that this layer is above the Special layer. The remaining objects you draw should be placed on this layer.

7) Draw a small circle above the i in Special.

You want the circle to cover the dot over the i.

8) Make 11 copies of the circle by holding Alt (Windows) or Option (Macintosh) as you drag the first circle. Place the new copies of the circle in an arc, moving from the *i* to the right of the text.

The circles will animate from left to right, in the order you create them.

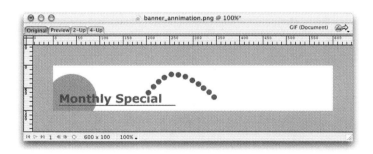

9) Select all of the circles. Choose Window > Frames to open the Frames panel.

The Frames panel displays each frame of the animation. Perhaps you remember flip books from your childhood. As you flipped through each page, the cartoon images appeared to move. The Frames panel simulates the pages in a flip book. Each frame contains a different view of the animation. The next step copies the circles and places each one in a separate frame.

⊙ POWER TIP *All of the circles are on the Animation layer. You can quickly select all of the circles by clicking the Animation layer on the Layers panel.*

10) Click Distribute to Frames on the Frames panel or choose this option from the Options pop-up menu.

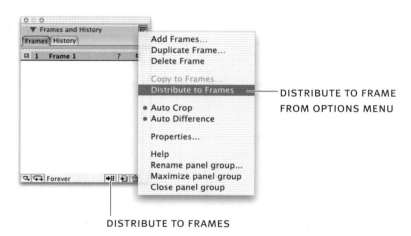

You should now have 12 frames displayed on the Frames panel. Placing the objects on the page before distributing them makes it easier to see the relationship of each circle to the next circle in the animation.

TIP *The stacking order of the objects on the layer determines the placement of the objects in the Frames panel. For example, the bottommost object (the first one you drew) is placed in Frame 1. If you want to add a new circle in the middle of the arc, then move its object on the Layers panel to the position you want it to appear in the animation.*

11) Click the Play/Stop VCR control button at the bottom of the document window to preview the animation.

The animation displays each circle object as the circles move across the canvas. The animation loops, continuing to play, until you click the control button again. You'll change the speed of the animation later in this lesson.

You can also click each frame on the Frames panel to view successive frames of the animation, or press Control + Page Up/Down (Windows) or Command + Page Up/Down (Macintosh) to move through the frames.

PLAY / STOP ANIMATION

USING ONION SKINNING

Onion skinning is a traditional animation technique that enables you to see and manipulate objects before and after the current frame. When you are creating frame-by-frame animation, this helps you position objects in each frame without flipping back and forth between frames. When onion skinning is turned on, objects in frames before and after the current frame are dimmed so you can distinguish them from objects in the current frame.

In the preceding exercise, you placed circles in an arc to simulate them shooting out from the dot in the *i*. After you play your animation, suppose you decide you want to move one of the circles to change the shape of the arc. When you select a frame, you can't see the circles in other frames, and so in the next exercise you will use onion skinning to reveal the contents of other frames.

1) Select Frame 1 on the Frames panel.

You can turn on onion skinning for selected frames or for all of the frames. The onion skinning marker is located in the left column of the Frames panel.

ONION SKINNING MARKER

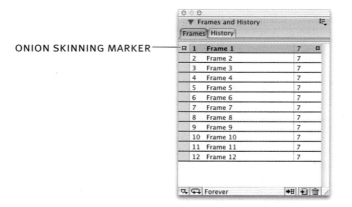

2) Click the left column of Frame 12.

A vertical bar appears in the left column, indicating that onion skinning is on for the frames.

ONION SKINNING BAR

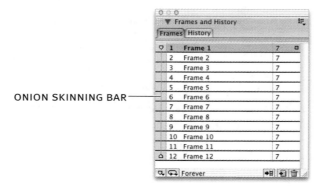

You can also control onion skinning from the Onion Skinning pop-up menu. Open it by clicking the button in the lower left corner of the Frames panel.

ONION SKINNING MENU

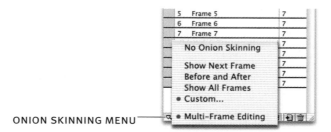

3) Choose Custom from the Onion Skinning pop-up menu to change the opacity of the frames before and after the current frame.

Onion skinning changes the opacity level of all frames other than the selected frame. You can use the Custom setting to change the opacity level. Setting the opacity level to 0 hides the contents; setting the opacity level to 100 makes the contents appear as if they are in the current frame.

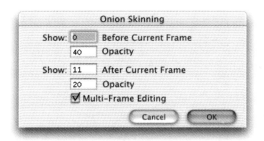

Choose Multi-Frame Editing to enable other frames to be selected and edited (even though they are dimmed).

With onion skinning on, you can now position your objects on the canvas. You can even move the dimmed circles on other frames while you are in this mode.

NOTE *Onion skinning is turned off when you play the animation using the VCR controls.*

SHARING A LAYER

When you play your animation, you see the Monthly Special text in the first frame, and then you see each small circle as it moves in an arc from left to right. The text, the large circle, and the line don't animate, but you want them to appear in each frame of the animation.

Instead of pasting all of the objects into each frame, you will set the layer of those objects to be shared across every frame in the animation. After the layer is shared, you can modify the objects on the layer from any frame, and all of the frames will be updated. If you had pasted copies of the objects into each frame, you would instead have to modify each copy in each frame.

1) Select Frame 1 on the Frames panel.

This is the frame that contains the objects you want to share across the other frames.

2) Double-click the Special layer to open the Layer Name window. Select the Share Across Frames option. Click outside the window to close it.

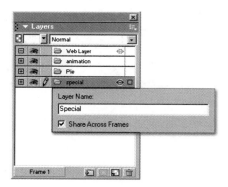

3) An alert box opens warning you that objects will be deleted in other frames. Click OK.

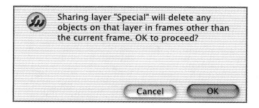

When you share a layer, any objects on that layer in other frames are deleted. In this exercise, the items you want to share are in Frame 1. If you had selected any frame other than Frame 1 before sharing the layer, then your items would be deleted from that frame. As long as you select the frame with the items you want to use before sharing the layer, you can ignore the warning.

After you click OK, everything on this shared layer is placed in all frames in your animation automatically. Any changes you make to elements on this layer will be reflected in all of the frames.

TIP *You can easily see which layers have the Share Layer option selected. Look at the Special layer on the Layers panel. It displays an icon to indicate this option.*

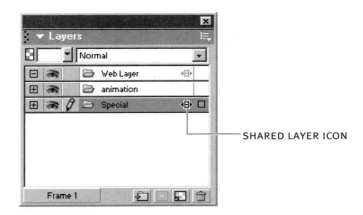

SHARED LAYER ICON

USING ANIMATION SYMBOLS

If you want control over every object in each frame of your animation, you must create your animation using the frame-by-frame animation method as you did in the first exercise. If you only need to make an object move across the canvas, you can create an animation symbol that makes the task much easier. An animation symbol adds a bounding box and a motion path to the symbol that indicates the direction that the symbol moves. You can change a variety of features, from the animation speed to the opacity and rotation. In this exercise, you will create an animation in which an object fades in.

1) Create a new layer and name it *Pie*.

Make sure that this layer is above the other layers.

TIP *Select the top layer before adding the new layer. This way your new layer is added at the top and you don't have to move it.*

2) Click the Options pop-up menu at the top right of the Frames panel; then choose Add Frames.

You need another frame to add more to the animation. Choose At the end in the Add Frames dialog box and add one frame at the end of your animation. Click OK.

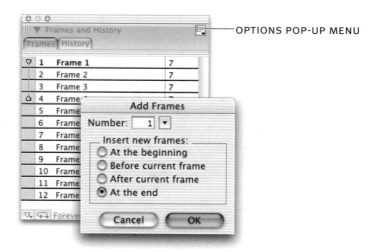

3) Select Frame 13 on the Frames panel.

The frame contains only the objects on the shared layer.

4) Import the *Strawberry_pie.png* image from the Media folder in the Lesson09 folder and place it to the right of the canvas. With the Text tool, type *Fresh Strawberry Pie, $9.95* and place the text to the left of the pie.

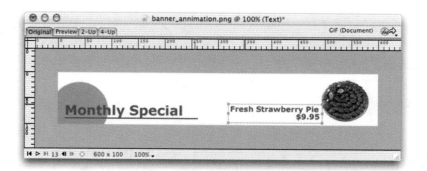

Change the font and size of the text so it fits on the page. You can use the red color for the text or choose your own color.

5) Turn on onion skinning to see the previous frame and place the text just to the right of the last circle in the animation.

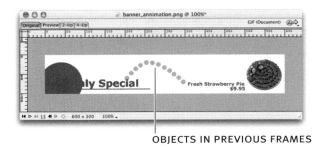

OBJECTS IN PREVIOUS FRAMES

6) With the text block and the pie image selected, choose Modify > Animation > Animate Selection. In the Animate dialog box, change the number of frames to 12, set Move (Windows) or Movement (Macintosh) to zero, and change the opacity to zero in the first Opacity settings box. Click OK.

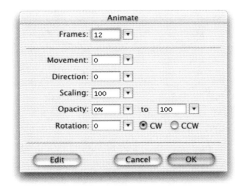

In the dialog box that opens, you are warned that the number of new frames extends beyond the last frame in this document.

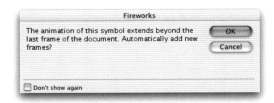

7) Click OK.

You want to add those extra frames.

You should now see the text block and the image surrounded by a dotted square, indicating that it is a symbol. The dotted square should have a red dot in the middle, indicating that it is an animation symbol.

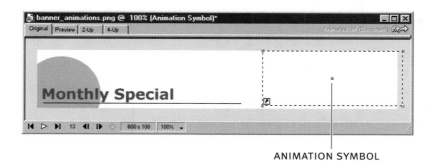

ANIMATION SYMBOL

8) Save your file and then click Play/Stop at the bottom of the document window to preview the animation.

The circles animate from left to right, and then the pie image and text fade in.

NOTE *The red dot in the middle of the animation symbol can be used to move the object on the canvas. You drag the red dot away from the symbol. The animation line that appears indicates the path of the animation. In this example, you want the image to remain in place, changing the opacity from 0 to 100 percent instead of moving the object.*

TIP *You can change the number of frames, scaling, rotation, or opacity of the animation symbol as it moves along the motion path. Select the symbol and then modify the settings in the Property inspector.*

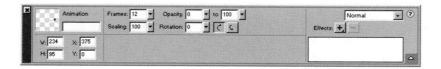

CONTROLLING PLAYBACK

Once you have the animation sequence working, you can change the playback speed by setting the frame delay. The frame delay determines the amount of time each frame is displayed. Frame delay is specified in hundredths of a second. For example, a setting of 100 displays the frame for a second, and a setting of 25 displays the frame for a quarter of a second. For the fastest animations, set the frame delay to zero.

1) Click Frame 1 on the Frames panel to select the first frame. Hold down Shift and click the last frame to select all of the frames in the animation.

You can change the frame delay for each frame individually or for all frames at once.

2) Access the Frames Option menu and choose Properties from the list.

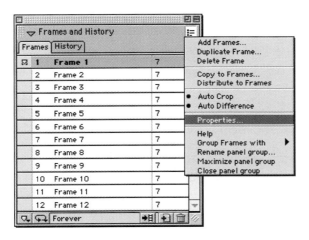

TIP *You can also double-click the selected frame to display the properties for that frame. Double-click the frame delay column (the right column), not the frame name. You can rename each frame; double-clicking the name enables you to type a new name. If multiple frames are selected, double-click one frame-delay column. The value you enter for the frame delay is applied to each of the selected frames.*

3) Type *10* in the Frame Delay text box. Click outside the Frame Properties pop-up window to close the window.

The smaller the number, the faster the animation plays.

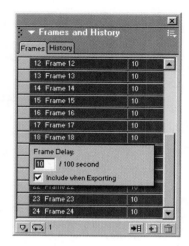

4) Click the Play/Stop control button to view the speed of your animation.

Repeat step 3 with a different frame delay if the animation is too fast or too slow.

Next you will set the looping control for your animation. Looping makes the animation play over and over. Make sure that looping your animation is absolutely necessary before you change this setting. There is nothing more irritating on a Web page than an animated GIF image that loops for no apparent reason. Make sure that the last frame of your animation contains the final information you want to display, and that you limit the number of loops.

5) Click the Looping button on the Frames panel if you want the animation to play more than once.

On the pop-up menu that opens, you can choose the number of times that you want the animation to loop. The number you choose does not include the first sequence of the animation; you'll actually see one more loop than the number you choose here. To remove the looping, choose No Looping.

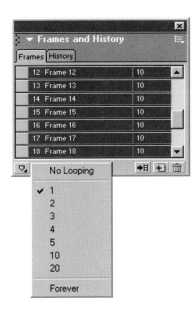

NOTE   *When you play your animation with the Play/Stop control button, it continues to loop regardless of your loop setting.*

6) Save your file.

EXPORTING A GIF ANIMATION

Once you have your animation the way you want it, you need to export it as an animated GIF file. You want to make sure that the file size is as small as possible, just as you do for the other images on your page. The more frames and colors in your animation, the larger the file size.

1) Choose Window > Optimize to access the Optimize panel. Choose Animated GIF Websnap 128 from the Settings pop-up menu.

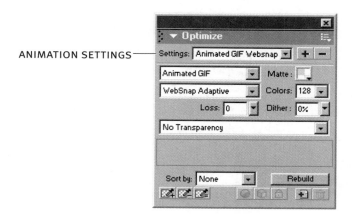

ANIMATION SETTINGS

Make any changes to the number of colors or other options on the Optimize panel as you learned in Lesson 8. View the images on the Preview panel to make sure that your color choices appear the way you want.

NOTE *If you don't select Animated GIF as the export file format on the Optimize panel, your file is exported as a static GIF file and will not animate. The preset Animated GIF WebSnap 128 option sets this file format for you.*

2) When you are satisfied with the settings, choose File > Export to export the file. Select Images Only from the Save As options and then click Save.

222

USING THE EXPORT PREVIEW WITH ANIMATIONS

The default settings for animated GIF files will work for most of your animations. If you need to tweak the settings, use the Export Preview command. You can set any number of loops, change the frame disposal method, and even hide a frame from view. The disposal method specifies what happens to the previous frame after the current one is displayed. The disposal method works only with transparency, so if your frames aren't transparent, you don't have to worry about it.

This section is for your reference only. Your current animation does not need changing.

1) Choose File > Export Preview to access the Export Preview window. Choose Animated GIF from the Format pop-up menu.

The Export Preview window displays three tabs for setting export options: Options, File, and Animations. The Options tab displays the same information as the Optimize panel. You can make changes here or use the Optimize panel.

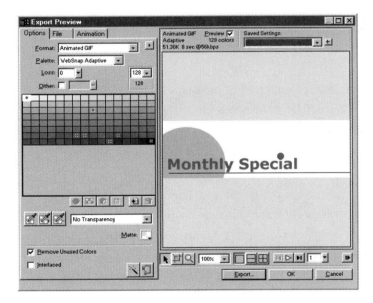

2) Click the Animation tab.

The Animation tab displays the frames in the animation, similar to the Frames panel, but with additional options.

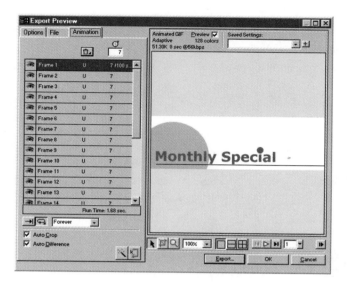

3) Select a frame on the Animation panel. Click the Disposal Method button (the trash can icon) and pick a method from the pop-up menu.

- **Unspecified**: No disposal method is specified. Fireworks automatically selects the disposal method for each frame. Choose Unspecified to create the smallest possible animated GIF file.

- **None**: The frame is not disposed of before the new frame is displayed. The next frame appears on top of the current frame. Choose None to add a smaller object to the existing frame.

- **Restore to Background**: This option erases the current frame's image and restores the area to the background color or pattern that appears in the Web browser. Choose Restore to Background when moving an object in a transparent animated GIF file.

- **Restore to Previous**: This option erases the current frame's image and restores that area to the previous frame's image. Choose Restore to Previous to animate objects across a background image.

224

Here are some guidelines: For full-frame animations, use Unspecified or None (frames overwrite each other). For frame optimization and transparency, use None (each new frame overlays the previous frame). To move frames within a larger frame, use Restore to Background to avoid multiple images.

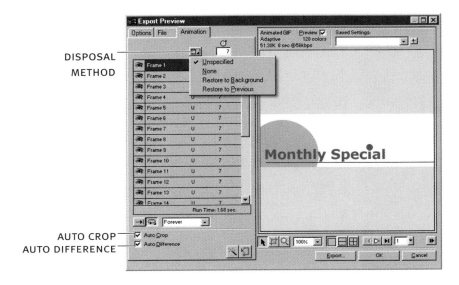

You don't need to worry about the disposal settings. Fireworks automatically selects the best method for your animation. Leave Disposal set to Unspecified, the default.

On the Animation tab, you can also turn off individual frames in the animation.

Use Auto Crop to crop each frame in the animation as a rectangular area so that only the image area that differs in each frame is output. Use Auto Difference to output only the pixels that change between frames. Both of these default options reduce the file size of the animation. If your animation looks bad or plays poorly, you might want to deselect these options to see if your animation improves.

4) Select a frame on the Animation panel. Click Show/Hide Frame (the eye) next to each frame to turn that frame on or off.

If a frame is turned off, it is not visible when you preview the animation in Fireworks, and it will not be exported with the animation.

225

5) When your settings are complete and the preview of the animation is to your liking, click Export. Name your file. The .gif extension is added automatically. Choose Images Only from the Save As pop-up options and then click Save.

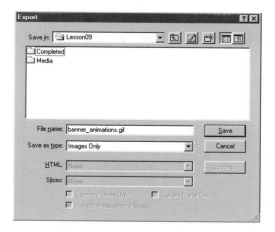

APPLYING TWEENING

Tweening is the process of defining beginning and ending frames and then creating images in between to give the appearance that the first frame slowly changes to the last frame. This is similar to tweening in Macromedia Flash. You define the first image as a symbol, make a copy of the symbol, and then let Fireworks calculate (tween) the images in the middle.

In this exercise, you look at different effects you can achieve by tweening.

1) Create a new document 100 by 100 pixels with a white canvas. Select the Polygon tool. In the Property inspector, change the shape to a five-pointed star; then draw a star on the canvas. Add an inner bevel to the star.

You can select the number of sides and the angle for either the Polygon shape or the Star shape.

2) With the star selected, choose Modify > Symbol > Convert to Symbol. In the Symbol Properties dialog box, select Graphic as the symbol type and then click OK.

You don't need to name the symbol.

3) Choose Edit > Clone. Then choose Modify > Transform > Rotate 180°.

You now have an exact copy of the symbol placed on top of the original. The clone is selected and will be rotated.

4) Choose Edit > Select All.

Both copies are selected. Look at the title bar of your document. The title bar displays the number of selected objects. You should see (2 objects) as part of the title bar. This indicator is very handy when you need to verify what you have selected.

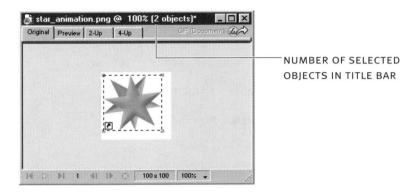

NUMBER OF SELECTED
OBJECTS IN TITLE BAR

NOTE *You may need to enlarge the document window to see the full title bar.*

5) Choose Modify > Symbol > Tween Instances. Enter *10* as the number of steps and select Distribute to Frames. Click OK.

The original star is the beginning point, and the rotated clone of the star is the ending point. Tweening creates new instances (copies) of the star based on the number of steps you enter. Distribute to Frames places the copies in new frames. If you forget to check the Distribute to Frames option, all of the stars are placed in Frame 1.

6) View the animation by clicking the Play/Stop button in the document window. You can close this file without saving.

TWEENING EFFECTS

You can also tween effects as part of the animation. For example, the star you just tweened had an inner bevel. You could create a star animation that started with a smooth edge and changed to a star with a bevel. The star would appear to morph from one shape to the other.

1) Create a new document 100 by 100 pixels with a white canvas. Select the Polygon tool and then draw a star on the canvas. Choose Modify > Symbol > Convert to Symbol. Click OK to close the Symbol Properties dialog box.

For this animation, you want to add the bevel to the symbol.

NOTE *The Polygon tool should still be set to a five-pointed star from the previous exercise. If not, you'll need to change the setting in the Property inspector.*

2) Add an inner bevel to the star and then add a drop shadow.

For this first symbol, change the width of the bevel to zero and change the drop shadow distance to zero and the opacity to zero. This applies the effect, but you can't see it.

3) Choose Edit > Clone.

For the clone, increase the inner bevel width and increase the drop shadow distance and opacity amount.

TIP *The same effects must be applied to both instances of the symbol. Changing the settings to zero allows you to apply the effect to the first instance without making it visible.*

4) Select both star symbols. Choose Modify > Symbol > Tween Instances. Enter *10* as the number of steps and select Distribute to Frames. Click OK. Click the Play/Stop button to preview the animation.

The star morphs from the first shape to the second one. The effects you applied are also animated.

5) You can close this file without saving.

WHAT YOU HAVE LEARNED

In this lesson, you have:

- Created a simple frame-by-frame animation [pages 208–210]

- Used onion skinning to modify the frames in the animation [pages 211–213]

- Shared a layer's elements across all frames in the animation [pages 214–215]

- Created an animation symbol [pages 215–218]

- Changed the playback speed and set the number of loops [pages 219–221]

- Exported the animation [pages 222–226]

- Used tweening to fade in an object [pages 226–227]

- Used tweening on the effects of an object [page 228]

masking and pop-up menus

In this lesson, you will build a new Web page using the buttons and the logo from your home page as a starting point. Then you will import an image and use masking to fit the image within a shape. You used Paste Inside in Lesson 2; you'll use another method in this lesson. Then, on another new page based on the home page, you will add pop-up menus to give additional navigation functionality to the page.

This is an example of the page you will build in this lesson.

WHAT YOU WILL LEARN

In this lesson, you will:

- Create a base template for your pages
- Use Paste as Mask to isolate an image
- Paint on a mask
- Use text as a mask
- Create a text slice
- Add a pop-up menu
- Edit the pop-up menu

APPROXIMATE TIME

This lesson takes approximately 2 hours to complete.

LESSON FILES

Media Files:

Lesson10\Media\founder.psd

Lesson10\Media\candy_corn_large.png

Lesson10\Media\clipboard.png

Lesson10\Media\gingerbread_house_small.png

Lesson10\Media\recipe_box.png

Lesson10\Media\mug.png

Lesson10\Media\buy.png

Lesson10\Media\about.txt

Lesson10\Media\facts.txt

Lesson10\Media\music.txt

Starting Files:

Lesson10\Start\about.png

Lesson10\Start\home_page_L10.png

Completed Projects:

Lesson10\Completed\about.png

Lesson10\Completed\facts.png

Lesson10\Completed\home_page_L10.png

Lesson10\Completed\music.png

Lesson10\Completed\shop.png

Lesson10\Completed\template.png

CREATING A TEMPLATE

In this exercise, you will create a new page, using the top portion of the home page you've been creating. You want to use this top portion for other pages of your site, so you will save that new page as a template that you can use for the other pages as well. Then you will mask an image for use on that page.

1) Open the home_page.png file you've been working on in the previous lessons.

If you no longer have that file, you can use the home_page_L10.png file in the Start folder within the Lesson10 folder.

2) Choose File › Save As and rename the file *template.png*. Delete all of the objects on the page except for the top red rectangle, the candy logo and stick, and the buttons.

Template page with only the base images on the page

Remember that you added 12 frames and placed images on those frames. You need to delete the product images on Frames 2 through 3. Then you can delete Frames 4 through 13. The first three frames contain the rollover images for your buttons, so you need to leave those in the document.

232

3) Hold down Shift as you select each frame you want to delete and then click the trash can button at the bottom right of the Frames panel.

You can also select Frame 4 and then hold down Shift and select the last frame. With all of the frames selected, you can then click the trash can button and delete all of the frames at once.

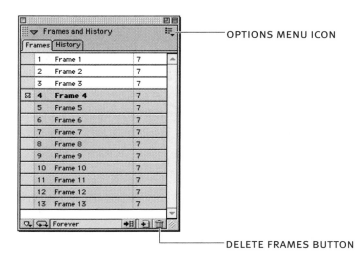

OPTIONS MENU ICON

DELETE FRAMES BUTTON

NOTE *You could also use the Options menu on the Frames panel to delete the frames, but clicking the trash can button is quicker.*

4) Save your template file; then choose File > Save As and name this new file *about.png*.

You will use the template file for other pages of your site. You will now work with the about.png file, adding a mask and some text. Make sure you select Frame 1 for the remaining exercises in this lesson.

MASKING AN IMAGE

Masking is a method of using the shape and the fill of one object to control another object. A mask can be either a vector or a bitmap. In Lesson 2, you used Paste Inside to place the triangles around the inside edge of the candy logo. Paste Inside is a form of masking: the circle controls how much of the image is displayed.

Another form of masking uses the fill of an object, not just the outline of the object. Imagine a piece of black construction paper with a hole cut from the middle. Place the construction paper over a picture. As you move the picture behind the paper, only a part of the picture is visible through the hole. The construction paper is acting as a mask. The size and shape of the cutout area determine what part of the picture is visible.

The color of the hole controls the visibility of the image. In the construction paper example, the cutout area is white, and so all the colors of the picture are displayed. If you place a piece of frosted glass over the picture, you see fewer colors in the picture because the frosted glass filters out some of the colors.

If the color of the mask is white, you see all of the colors of the image beneath the mask. If the color of the mask is black, the entire image is hidden. Shades of gray show varying amounts of the image.

1) Select the Specials layer on the Layers panel.

You want the new objects for this page on that layer. If you want, you can lock the other layers to make sure the elements on those layers are not accidentally moved or deleted.

2) From within the about.png file, choose File > Import. Open the founder.psd file in the Media folder within the Lesson10 folder.

Click to place the image on the page. (The image is an Adobe Photoshop file.) You want to round the corners of the image and crop it more tightly. To do this, you will create a mask.

3) Draw a rounded rectangle, 124 by 134 pixels. Change the roundness to about 30. Make the rectangle with a thin black stroke and a fill of None.

You want the fill to be set to None so you can see the image of the founder as you complete the next step.

4) Resize the image by using the Scale tool or holding down Shift as you drag a corner handle with the Pointer tool.

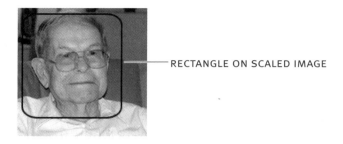 ──── RECTANGLE ON SCALED IMAGE

Scale the image so it is slightly larger than the rectangle. You want the face of the founder to fit within the rectangle. You can move the rectangle over the image before you scale the image to help determine the size you need. If you make the image too small, don't make it larger. Instead, choose Edit > Undo Transform to reverse the scaling changes and try again. Remember that you can make a bitmap image smaller, but if you make it larger, you reduce the quality of the image.

5) Select the rectangle with the Pointer tool and then choose Edit > Cut. Select the image and then choose Edit > Paste as Mask.

The image is placed within the rectangle. The Paste as Mask command with a vector object creates a vector mask that crops the masked object using the outline of the vector object. Select the masked image, and you see a star—the move handle—in the middle of the image. You can drag the move handle to move the image around in the mask. (You are moving the image within the mask, not the object itself. To move the image object, drag another part of the object.)

 ──── MOVE HANDLE IN MASK

235

The stroke on the rectangle disappeared when you made it a mask. In the next step, you will show the stroke. Look on the Specials layer for the masked object. The image and the mask appear together as a group. The icon for the mask is on the right (it contains a small pen, indicating that it is a vector mask). The layer object is labeled Bitmap.

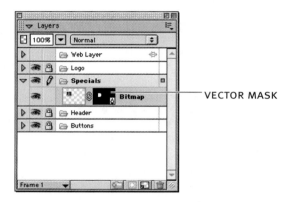

VECTOR MASK

6) Click the mask icon on the Layers panel.

When you select the mask icon, a yellow border appears around the icon. The Property inspector displays options for the mask.

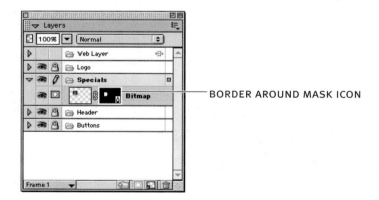

BORDER AROUND MASK ICON

236

7) Select Path Outline in the Property inspector and then select Show Fill and Stroke.

The stroke appears on the rectangle. You can change the stroke settings for the mask in the Property inspector.

You want the masked image of the founder to the right of the candy stick. When you move the image, make sure you grab the image, not the move handle (the blue star).

8) Using the Text tool, type *ABOUT US*. Change the font to Arial Black, the color to the red color of the top rectangle, and the size to 75 points. Choose Modify > Transform > Rotate 90° CCW.

The text is rotated. Move the text to the right of the canvas. You can change the size if necessary to fit the text on your page.

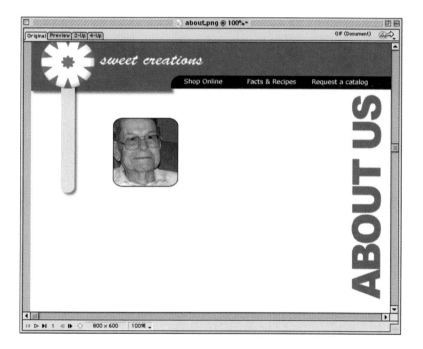

9) Save your file.

The next exercise shows you another masking technique. You will continue working with this same file.

MASKING USING THE LAYERS PANEL

Another method for creating a mask is to use the Layers panel. Using the Layers panel is a quick way to add a white bitmap mask to an image. Then you can use any of the bitmap tools to "paint" on the mask to customize its look.

1) Create a new document 400 by 400 pixels with a white canvas. Import the founder.psd image.

For this exercise, you will use the same founder image as you used in the previous exercise. Then you can choose which image you want to use on your About page.

2) Click Add Mask at the bottom of the Layers panel.

An empty mask is applied to the image. You see a mask thumbnail on the Layers panel. A yellow border around the mask thumbnail on the Layers panel indicates that it is selected.

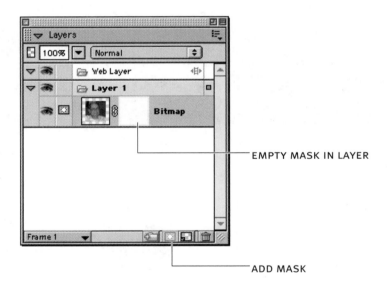

EMPTY MASK IN LAYER

ADD MASK

3) Select the Brush tool from the Tools panel. Click Set Default Stroke/Fill Colors on the Tools panel.

The default stroke color is set to black; the default fill color is set to white. The Property inspector displays the settings for the Brush tool. You can experiment with different strokes and brush sizes as you complete this step. For example, try Viscous Alien Paint from the Unnatural category for an interesting effect.

STROKE CATEGORY

4) Draw along the outside edge of the image.

Remember that you are actually painting on the mask. As you paint with black on the mask, you are hiding that portion of the image. (If you see black brush strokes, you are painting on the image, not the mask. Undo your brush strokes and then click the mask thumbnail on the Layers panel.) If you hide too much of the image, you can switch the stroke color to white and paint over the hidden area to reveal the image.

When you paint on the mask, you are altering the visibility of the masked image. Painting with white makes the masked image completely visible. Painting with black makes the masked area invisible. Painting on the mask with shades of gray makes the masked area partially visible. The lighter the shade of gray, the more you see of the image; the darker the shade, the less you see of the image.

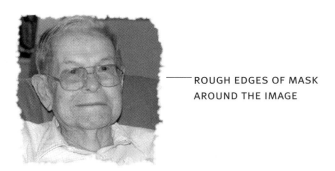

ROUGH EDGES OF MASK
AROUND THE IMAGE

TIP *You can press X to quickly swap the stroke and fill colors as you paint on the mask. This is the shortcut key for Swap Stroke and Fill colors on the Tools panel.*

5) When you achieve a look that you like, use the Scale tool to resize the image. You can replace the image of the founder on your About page with this image if you prefer. Save and close this file.

USING TEXT AS A MASK

Using text as a mask creates an interesting effect. You don't need it for this page, but you might want to experiment with the technique to see how it works.

1) Open the candy_corn_large.png file in the Media folder in the Lesson10 folder.

This is a larger version of the image you used for October in your disjointed rollover on the home page.

2) Select the Text tool and type *CANDY*. Change the font to Arial Black, change the color to white, and make the size large enough to fit over the candy image.

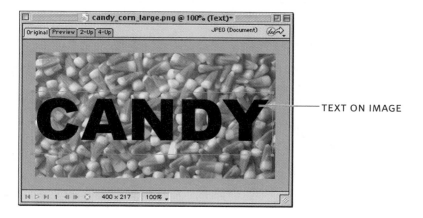

TEXT ON IMAGE

3) Select the text and choose Edit > Cut. Select the image and then choose Edit > Paste as Mask.

The candy corn image is placed within the outlines of the text.

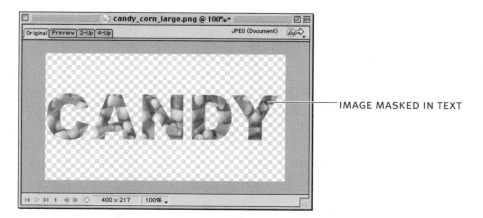

IMAGE MASKED IN TEXT

4) You can close this file without saving it.

CREATING A TEXT SLICE

The about.png file you have been working on will contain a brief history of the company founder. You could import the text for the page and format it as you did the text on the home page. However, this page contains more text, and you don't want it to be a graphic; remember that all text in Fireworks is converted to a graphic image when you export the page. Therefore, you will instead create a text slice that will export as text.

1) In your about.png file, choose File > Import and open the *about.txt* file in the Media folder within the Lesson10 folder. Click to place the text on the canvas.

The text will not remain on this page.

2) Using the Text Editor or the Text tool, select all of the text and copy it. Then delete the text block on the canvas.

You are importing the text just to copy it. You could have also opened the text file in a text editor such as NotePad or SimpleText and then copied the text.

3) Draw a slice on the canvas for the text, between the About Us text and the image of the founder. Also draw slices over the About Us text and the founder image.

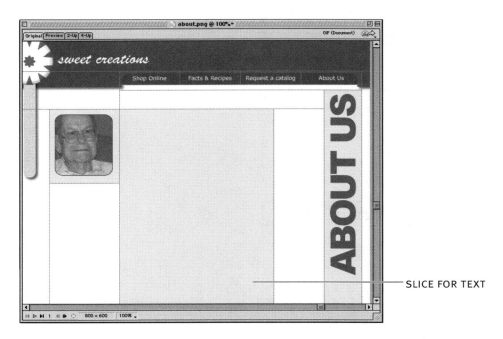

SLICE FOR TEXT

Don't overlap any of the slices. Use the red slice guides to help place the slices. Make the slice for the About Us text extend to the bottom of the canvas.

4) Add names for your slices over the founder and the About Us text.

You don't need to name the slice for the text; it won't be exported as a graphic.

5) Select the slice for the text and then select HTML from the Type pop-up menu in the Property inspector. Click the Edit button in the Property inspector.

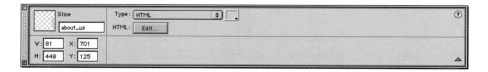

The HTML slice is a darker green color than the other slices. You can change the color of the slice by choosing a new color from the Color pop-up window on the Property inspector when the slice is selected.

6) Press Ctrl+V (Windows) or Command+V (Macintosh) to paste the text within the Edit HTML Slice window.

The File menu is not available when you are in the Edit HTML Slice window.

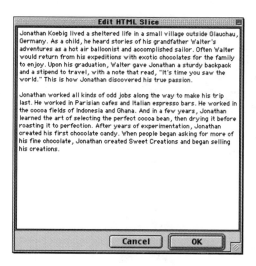

The text that appears in this window will be converted to HTML text when you export your page. This text consists of two paragraphs. If you leave it as is, the two paragraphs will be combined into one when you export your page. HTML requires tags surrounding all paragraphs or surrounding any words that you want to format. For example, if you want a word to appear in bold in the browser, you must place an opening bold tag () before the word and an ending bold tag () after the word.

You can enter the tags here in Fireworks, or you can make those changes in Dreamweaver. Even if you are not familiar with HTML, you can easily add the paragraph tags.

7) Type ‹p› before each paragraph and ‹/p› at the end of each paragraph; then click OK.

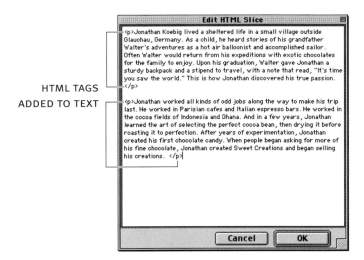

HTML TAGS
ADDED TO TEXT

If you want to add other HTML formatting tags, you can add them now as well.

8) Save and close your file.

You will export this page in the next lesson.

ADDING A POP-UP MENU

Pop-up menus are currently very popular on Web pages. A pop-up menu on a Web page is a navigation tool that is hidden until the user rolls over a button or an image on the page. Because the menus are initially hidden, you can pack a lot of links into a small space. You can also include submenus to add even more navigational links to your page. Hand-coding the JavaScript needed to create pop-up menus is tedious, but Fireworks makes the process as easy as entering names and links in a dialog box.

In this exercise, you will create a new page for the pop-up menus.

1) Open the template.png file you created earlier in this lesson. Choose File > Save As and name the new file *facts.png*. Select the Specials layer on the Layers panel and then import the recipe_box.png file from the Media folder in the Lesson10 folder. Import the clipboard file you created in Lesson 5.

You can use the clipboard.png file in the Media folder within the Lesson10 folder if you did not create one of your own. Rotate and scale the clipboard to fit on the page.

2) Draw a small rectangle and add the text *Chocolate Recipes*.

You can add a bevel to the rectangle to make it look more like a button. You don't need to use the Button Editor, as this button will not be a rollover button.

3) Group the text and the rectangle. Move the button over the image of the recipe box.

3) Select the button and then choose Edit > Insert > Slice.

To add the pop-up menu, you need to have a slice on the button object.

NOTE *Pop-up menus can be added to slices, hotspots, and button symbols.*

4) With the slice selected, choose Modify > Pop-up Menu > Add Pop-up Menu.

In the Pop-up Menu Editor, you enter the content for the menu: the text, the link, and the target for the link.

For this pop-up menu, you will have three categories of recipes: Cakes, Cookies, and Beverages. Then you will have submenus for each category.

TIP *You can also click the behavior handle on the slice and choose Add Pop-up Menu instead of choosing the option from the menu bar.*

5) Type *Cakes* in the Text column and then press Enter (Windows) or Return (Macintosh) to add a new line.

Cakes is the first category in your pop-up menu. It will not have a link.

6) Type *Chocolate Truffle Cake* in the Text column of the second row. Press Tab and then type *truffle.htm* as the link. Click the Indent Menu button to make this entry a submenu of Cakes.

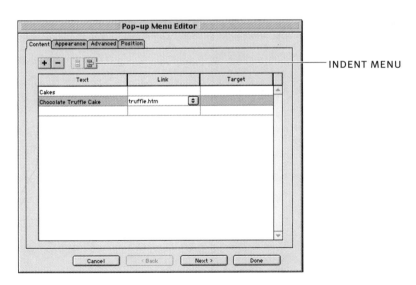

INDENT MENU

NOTE *The target setting is used when you have frames on your page or when you want to open the linked page in a new browser window; it is not needed for this exercise.*

8) Press Enter or Return again to add a new row. Type *Chocolate Mousse Cake* in the Text column, press Tab, and then type *mousse.htm* in the Link column. Continue in this fashion, adding text for the menus and submenus and adding links for the submenus. Enter text as shown in the following figure.

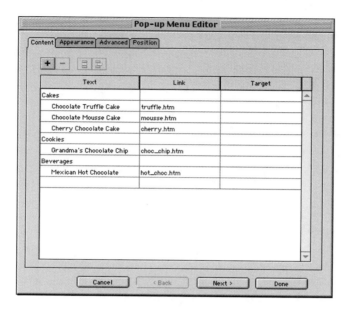

If you need to make changes to the text or the links, double-click the text to display the insertion bar and then make your changes.

NOTE *The Pop-up Menu Editor works like a spreadsheet. You press Tab to move to the next column. When you are in the last column, press Tab again to add a new row.*

9) Click Next (or click the Appearance tab) when you have entered all of the text and links.

On the Appearance tab, you can choose the look of the menus.

10) From the Up State options, choose the color of the text and cell when the item is initially displayed. From the Over State options, choose the color of the text and cell when the pointer is over the item.

The dialog box displays a preview of the pop-up menu.

NOTE *If you select Image for the Cells option, you create a GIF background image for the cells in the pop-up menu. If you select HTML for the Cells option, the pop-up menu is created with text and a background color for the table cell in the Up and Over states. For this exercise, use the HTML option.*

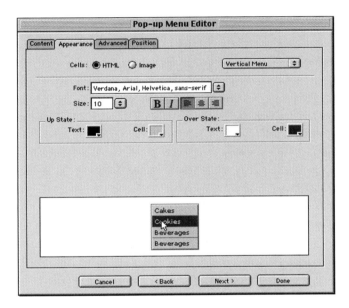

11) Click Next (or click the Advanced tab).

In this area, you can adjust the look of the text in the pop-up menu. For this exercise, you can leave the default options.

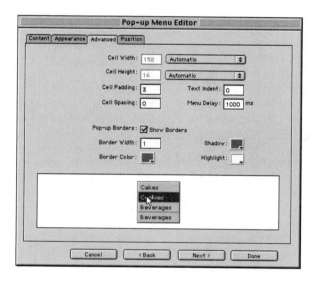

12) Click Next (or click the Position tab).

In this area, you can select the positions for the menu and submenu.

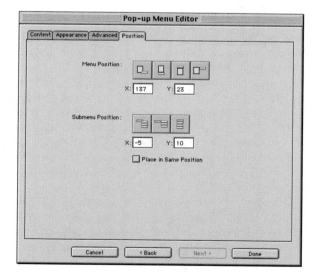

13) Click the first button for both the menu and submenu positions to set their positions to the bottom right of the slice; then click Done.

You'll see a blue line and a series of three blue rectangles that represent the pop-up menu. The position of the menu is based on the option you selected in this step. If you don't like the placement now that you see it on the page, you can move the menu. Move the pointer over one of the blue rectangles. The pointer changes to the pointing hand. When you see the hand pointer, you can drag the rectangle to place the pop-up menu where you want it to appear on the page.

14) Repeat from step 2 and add another button over the clipboard. Add the text *Chocolate Facts*. For the pop-up menu, add the text *Benefits* and *History*, with *benefits.htm* and *history.htm*, respectively, as the links.

You don't need a submenu for the Facts pop-up menu.

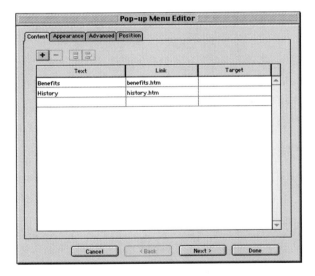

15) Save your file.

EDITING A POP-UP MENU

Once you complete your pop-up menu, you will want to see it in action. The pop-up menu does not appear in the Fireworks preview window. You must preview in the browser to see the pop-up menu.

Before you preview the file, you need to take a few steps to make sure that Fireworks knows how to export your file. Even though you are only previewing the file, Fireworks is creating temporary images and the necessary HTML.

1) Choose File > HTML Setup.

You modified the settings in this dialog box in Lesson 8. For this file, you need to check the settings on the Document Specific tab.

2) Click the Document Specific tab. Select Include Areas without Slices.

This ensures that all of the objects are exported, even if you haven't drawn a slice over an object.

3) In the File Names for Slices area, set the pop-up menus to doc.name, Underscore, and Slice #(01,02,03...) and set the Frames to Underscore and Frame# (f2, f3, f4), or any other naming option from the pop-up menu. Click OK.

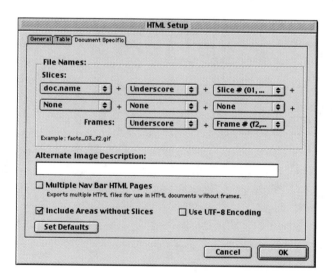

NOTE *If you don't set the format for the HTML, you may see repeating patterns of the same image when you preview the page. Choosing a naming format for the slices ensures that each slice has a distinct name.*

4) Choose File > Preview in Browser.

Check your pop-up menus and submenus in the browser. When you roll over the button, the pop-up menu appears. The links won't work in the browser until you export your file.

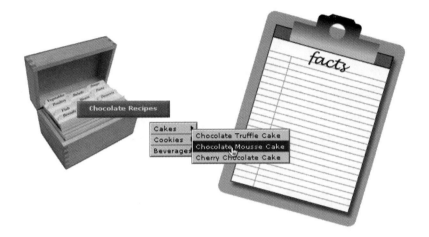

If you want to make a change to the items in your pop-up menu or add new items to the list, select the slice on the button and then double-click within the blue rectangles of the pop-up menu. If you don't see the slices, click Show Slices and Hotspots on the Tools panel. The Pop-up Menu Editor dialog box appears, where you can make your changes.

ON YOUR OWN

Import the facts.txt text from the Media folder in the Lesson10 folder into the facts.png page you are working on in this lesson. Copy and paste that text onto an HTML slice on the page. You can delete the text block you imported. Then save your file.

In the next lesson, you will export all of the pages you have created and use Dreamweaver to make some changes to the pages. At this point, you have the Home page, the About page, and the Facts page. You are missing the Shop page that corresponds to the Shop Online button on your pages, and the Request page that corresponds to the Request a Catalog button. You also need to make a Music page. The guitar and CD you created in Lesson 5 go on this page.

NOTE *If you don't have the time to create these extra pages, you will find them in the Completed folder in the Lesson10 folder. They are also located in the Start folder in the Lesson11 folder.*

To create those pages, you need to open the template.png file you created and save that file with a new name as you did with the About page. For the Shop page, you need to build a navigation area for linking to the Music page. Then use the Hotspot tool to add a link to music.htm. Use the example here to build the Shop page, or add your own creative elements. The Media folder in the Lesson10 folder contains some images you can use for this page.

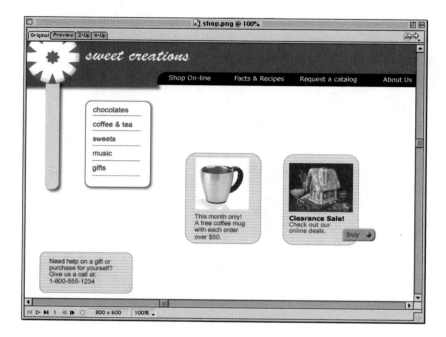

For the Music page, start again with the template.png file and save that file as music.png. Import the guitar and CD you created in Lesson 5. Grouping the elements of the guitar and CD after you import them makes them easier to manage and move on the page.

Use the following example to build the music page. Copy the navigation menu from the Shop page to this page. To make the CD cover, make a copy of the CD and place it on top of a colored square. Then scale both objects. The text for the CD description is in the music.txt file in the Media folder of the Lesson10 folder. Draw a slice over the CD and the guitar, a slice over the CD text, and a slice over the CD cover. Name the slice over the guitar and CD *instruments*, name the slice over the CD cover *cd_cover*, and name the slice over the text *cd_text*. Change the optimization for the guitar slice to JPEG. In the next lesson, you will re-optimize that image from Dreamweaver.

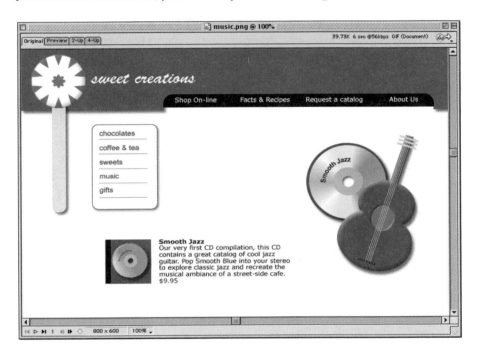

WHAT YOU HAVE LEARNED

In this lesson, you have:

- Created a template for the pages in the site [pages 232–233]
- Used masking to isolate a portion of an image [pages 234–237]
- Added a mask on the Layers panel and painted on the mask [pages 238–239]
- Used text as a mask for an image [page 240]
- Added a text slice [pages 241–243]
- Added pop-up menus for additional user interactivity [pages 244–249]
- Edited the pop-up menu [pages 250–251]

integrating with dreamweaver mx

LESSON 11

In the previous lessons, you used Fireworks to create a logo and other graphic elements such as the guitar and CD. You also designed several Web pages. Except in the few places where you added a text slice, your HTML pages are mostly images. More than likely, you will want to add text to your pages.

Macromedia Dreamweaver MX is a robust visual Web page authoring tool, and Macromedia Fireworks MX is a powerful design and graphics editor. Used together, Fireworks MX and Dreamweaver MX are the dynamic duo of Web design tools. The two programs offer integration features to aid your workflow as you design and optimize your graphics, build your HTML pages, and place Web graphics on the page.

In this lesson, you will use Dreamweaver MX to edit the pages created by Fireworks, return to Fireworks to change the graphics, and then return to Dreamweaver MX to make other edits. The tight integration between the two applications makes these tasks as simple as clicking a button.

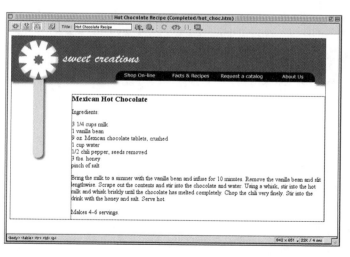

In this lesson you will export your pages as HTML files and then open them in Dreamweaver MX. You will create a Dreamweaver template and create new HTML pages from the template such as the page shown here.

WHAT YOU WILL LEARN

In this lesson, you will:

- Export your pages for Dreamweaver

- Create a local site in Dreamweaver

- View your pages in Dreamweaver

- Set Dreamweaver preferences

- Add links in Dreamweaver

- Edit a Fireworks page from Dreamweaver

- Create a Dreamweaver template

- Add text in Dreamweaver

- Edit a Fireworks pop-up menu

APPROXIMATE TIME

This lesson takes approximately 2 hours
to complete.

LESSON FILES

Media Files:

Lesson11\Media\benefits.txt
Lesson11\Media\cherry_choc_cake.txt
Lesson11\Media\choc_chip_cookies.txt
Lesson11\Media\choc_mousse_cake.txt
Lesson11\Media\history_short.txt
Lesson11\Media\hot_choc.txt
Lesson11\Media\truffle_cake.txt

Starting Files:

Lesson11\Start\about.png
Lesson11\Start\facts.png
Lesson11\Start\home_page.png
Lesson11\Start\music.png
Lesson11\Start\shop.png
Lesson11\Start\template.png

Completed Projects:

Lesson11\Completed\about.htm
Lesson11\ Completed\facts.htm
Lesson11\ Completed\home_page.htm
Lesson11\ Completed\music.htm
Lesson11\ Completed\shop.htm
Lesson11\ Completed\template.htm
Lesson11\ Completed\hot_choc.htm

FIREWORKS MX AND DREAMWEAVER MX

Generally, you will use Fireworks MX to create your Web graphics, and you will use Dreamweaver MX to build the Web pages. However, on pages with extensive graphics, you may prefer to use Fireworks as the design tool, exporting the HTML table structure as you did in the previous lessons. Rollovers created in Fireworks appear as native Dreamweaver behaviors when the resulting file is opened in Dreamweaver, ensuring a seamless workflow between the two applications. You can modify the Fireworks-generated table in Dreamweaver to add text or images. If a graphic needs updating, you can edit the image from within Dreamweaver. Dreamweaver launches Fireworks automatically so you can make the changes. Fireworks replaces only the HTML and image slice files needed to update the Dreamweaver file. Any changes you make in Dreamweaver are preserved.

When you launch Dreamweaver, you'll see some familiar interface features. Fireworks and Dreamweaver share a common Macromedia user interface that makes using these two programs together even easier. The common interface reduces the learning curve and increases your productivity. Icons and panels, where appropriate, have the same look and feel. For example, the Behaviors panels in Fireworks and Dreamweaver have the same icons and appearance.

Customizable keyboard shortcuts enable designers to configure both products to fit their personal design workflow. If you are accustomed to shortcuts from another graphics program—Macromedia FreeHand, for example—you can change Fireworks to use the same shortcuts. Again, the learning curve is reduced, giving you more time to design and produce your Web pages.

The communication between Fireworks and Dreamweaver occurs as comments in the HTML code and in Design Notes. Design Notes are like sticky notes attached to your HTML files. The information in the notes appears only within the Dreamweaver application—it is not in the HTML or placed on the server. If you are working with a team on a site, you can share information about the status of a file with Design Notes.

Fireworks saves the file name and path name of the original PNG source file in a Design Note when you have Design Notes enabled in Dreamweaver. When you save and export a Fireworks file within a Dreamweaver site, Fireworks creates a _notes folder and Design Note (a file ending with .mno) describing the file. Save your Fireworks original graphics (the PNG files) in a folder within a Dreamweaver site to maximize the integration between the two applications.

EXPORTING YOUR PAGES FOR DREAMWEAVER

In Lesson 8, you learned how to set the optimization for slices and export your pages as HTML. At this point, you have exported only one of the pages, and you saved the exported files in the Lesson08 folder. That was fine for learning the exporting process, but now you want to export all of your pages and create a cohesive Web site. The Web site referred to in this book is the local storage location of your files. Typically, you store your files in a folder on your local disk. Within that folder, you can then create subfolders to further organize your files. For example, you can put product pages in one folder and company information in another. In this exercise, you will export all of your Fireworks files and save them in a folder.

NOTE *Organizing your files in a folder enables you to easily upload your files to the Web server. You can then copy the entire folder to the Web server, or you can use the FTP feature in Dreamweaver to upload the files to the Web server.*

1) Open the home_page.png file you completed in Lesson 7.

If you no longer have that file, you can open the home_page.png file in the Start folder within the Lesson11 folder.

Before exporting your files, you need to check several things:

- Check that your slices have the proper optimization settings (as discussed in Lesson 8). Remember that each slice can be optimized differently.
- Check that your slices have names assigned. The name of the slice determines the name for the exported image. For example, if you set GIF as the optimization format for a slice and the slice name is candy, then the name of the exported file is candy.gif. Slices without names are assigned the file name. The settings you assign in the HTML Setup dialog box control the suffix of the file name. For example, if you use the settings shown in the following figure, then the file names for unnamed slices in the about.png file would be about_01.gif, about_02.gif, and so on.

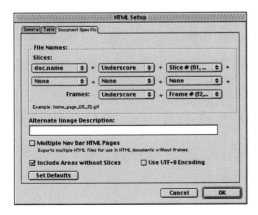

- Confirm that the option Include Areas without Slices is checked so that the entire page is exported to HTML. The areas without slices are exported using the naming scheme you assign in the HTML Setup dialog box, as described in the preceding paragraph.

2) Choose File > Export. Navigate to the HTML folder in the Lessons folder.

For this exercise, you will export all of the files to this folder and place the images in the Images folder. Verify the file name for your HTML file. For this exercise, make sure the name is home_page.htm.

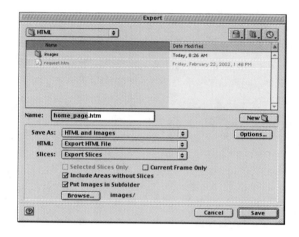

NOTE *The HTML folder already contains a file (request.htm). You will use this file later in this lesson.*

3) Repeat steps 1 and 2 for your about.png, facts.png, music.png, shop.png, and template.png files.

Check the HTML setup for each file and use about.htm for the About page, facts.htm for the Facts page, music.htm for the Music page, shop.htm for the Shop page, and template.htm for the template file.

NOTE *Your files were created by making a copy of your home page file. The default name for the HTML file is that original name. Make sure to check the HTML file name for each file you export. Also, the top portion (the logo, the buttons, the stick, and the header) should be exactly the same in each document. Similarly, the slices and the names of each slice in the top portion of each document should be the same. When you export the next file, you will receive a warning that an image exists and asking if you want to replace that file. Since all of your slices for the top portion are the same, click OK to replace the file.*

CREATING A LOCAL SITE IN DREAMWEAVER

Once all of the HTML files are exported, you are ready to open Dreamweaver MX, create a site, and begin modifying your pages. In Dreamweaver MX, you will notice a familiar user interface. The panels dock and open just as they do in Fireworks MX. The Property inspector also works like it does in Fireworks, displaying information based on the currently selected object.

1) In Dreamweaver MX, choose Site > New Site.

In the Site Definition dialog box, you can click either Basic or Advanced to define the site. The Basic tab (the Site wizard) steps you through the process of setting up the site. For this exercise, you'll use the wizard.

2) Click the Basic tab and then type a name for the site when the wizard asks what you want to name your site. For example, type *Sweet Creations* as the site name. Then click Next.

The name you enter is for your reference only. Make the name meaningful based on the content of the site. You may have multiple sites residing on your hard drive—for example, you may be creating Web pages for your company, school, church, or other organization—and each needs a unique name.

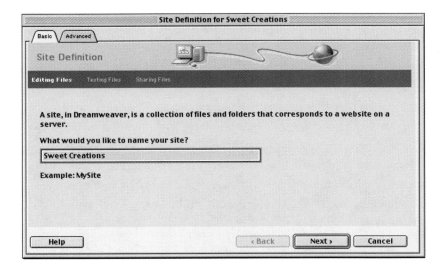

259

3) Select No, and then click Next.

In Dreamweaver MX, you can create a dynamic or a static site. A dynamic site uses a database to generate the content of a Web page. That concept is beyond the scope of this book. For this exercise, you will create a static site.

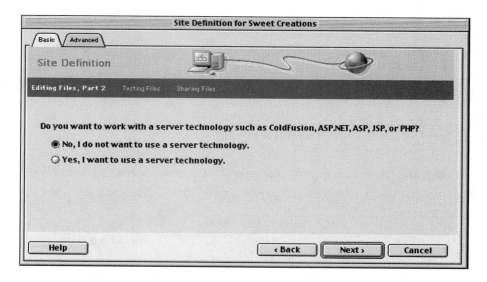

4) Select Edit Local Copies, and then click the folder icon and browse to the location of your Lessons folder. Click Next.

- For Windows: Open the local folder (the Lessons folder in this exercise) and click Select.

- For Macintosh: Select the local folder and click Choose.

After you define the main folder, it becomes the root folder for your site. All of your files and subfolders are contained within that root folder. Dreamweaver uses the local root folder to locate all links specified as site-root-relative URLs. When you create your pages, the graphics and links are relative to that folder. When you are ready to publish your site, all you have to do is copy the root folder and all of its files to the remote server. The images and links should all work on the Web server (assuming that they work locally).

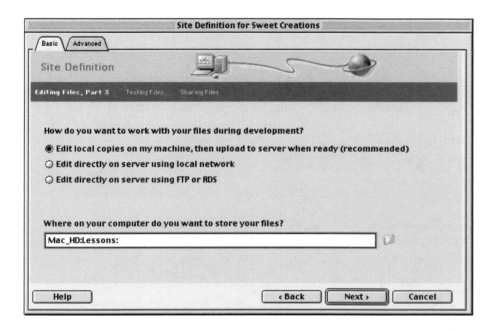

5) Choose None when asked the method for connecting to the remote server. Click Next.

For this exercise, you will not copy your files to a remote server. If you choose another option, you then are asked the method to use to connect to a remote server.

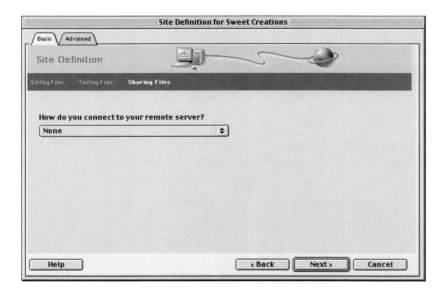

6) Click Done.

A summary of your settings is displayed. If you need to make a change, click the Back button and make the change.

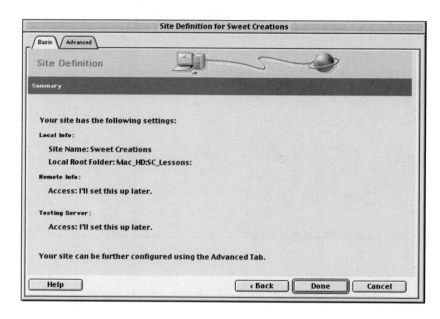

NOTE *You may see a message telling you that the site cache will be created. If you select Don't Show This Message Again, the message is skipped the next time you create a site. Click OK to close the message box and create the cache.*

You can also use the Advanced tab to define your site. When you click each item in the Category list, you are presented with the options for that category.

262

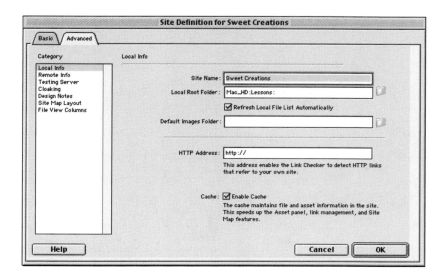

Local Info is where you define the site name as you did on the first screen of the Site wizard.

Remote Info is where you define the method for copying your files to the Web server.

Testing Server is where you define the server model for your site and the method of accessing the server.

Cloaking is where you can exclude folders or files from site operations. Simply enable cloaking and list the file types you want excluded. For example, the Fireworks PNG files you created don't need to be sent to the server. If you enable cloaking and then add the .png extension to the list, your Fireworks files will not be sent to the server. List all of the extensions you want excluded, separated by spaces.

NOTE *If you are using a Macintosh, make sure that you add the file name extension when you save your files. Many programs have an option you can select to add the extension automatically. If you are using Macromedia Flash, the extension is .fla; for Adobe Photoshop, the extension is .psd; and for Microsoft Word, the extension is .doc. Although the extension is not needed when you use the files on the Macintosh, it is necessary when you exchange your files with PC users. In addition, the extension is needed for the cloaking option in Dreamweaver.*

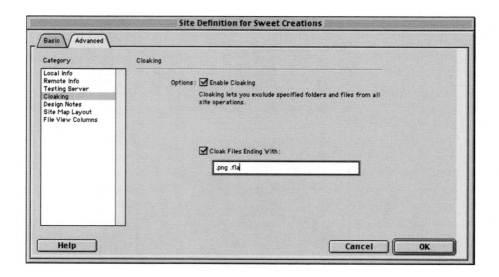

Design Notes are used for communication between Dreamweaver and Fireworks. Design Notes contain information about the graphic files when you export your files from Fireworks. When you export your files, Fireworks creates a folder called _notes and stores information about the files in that folder. When you edit a file from Dreamweaver, Dreamweaver uses that information to locate the source PNG file. If you are working with a team, you can select Upload Design Notes for Sharing. That option is not needed for this exercise.

Site Map Layout controls the look of a site map.

File View Columns controls the look of the Site panel.

VIEWING YOUR PAGES IN DREAMWEAVER

Once you define your site, you use the Site panel to manage the files. The Site panel displays files and folders at your local site and works similar to Windows Explorer or the Finder on the Macintosh. You should see the lesson folders and icon for your local hard drive (labeled Hard Disk in Windows and Computer on the Macintosh).

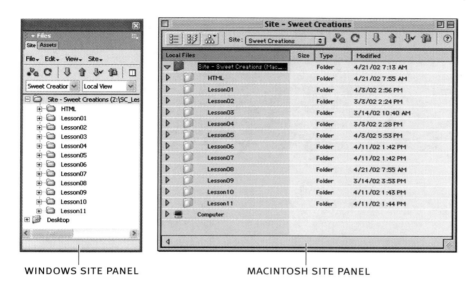

WINDOWS SITE PANEL   MACINTOSH SITE PANEL

1) On the Site panel, click the plus sign (Windows) or triangle (Macintosh) next to the HTML folder to reveal the folder's contents. Double-click your home_page.htm file in that folder.

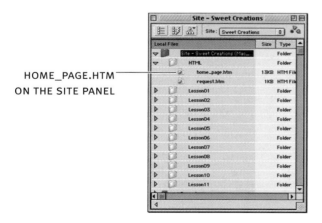

HOME_PAGE.HTM
ON THE SITE PANEL

Your home page opens. You should see all of the graphics you created in Fireworks. Click an image on the page. The Property inspector lists the image size. The size of the image corresponds to the slice you drew in Fireworks. The dotted line on the page represents the table that Fireworks built.

265

2) Type *Sweet Creations Home Page* in the Title text box at the top of the Document window.

Every HTML document should have a title. The title, used primarily for document identification, is displayed in a browser's title bar and is used as the bookmark name. Choose a short phrase that describes the document's purpose. The title can be of any length, but you may want to crop it if it's too long to fit in the browser title bar.

TITLE TEXT BOX IN THE DOCUMENT WINDOW

TIP *If you don't see the Title text box at the top of the Document window, choose View > Toolbars > Document.*

The title that Fireworks assigns is the default image name for your file: for example, home_page.gif. That name is not very descriptive. You should make checking the title name the first step when you open your files.

NOTE *If you create a new file in Dreamweaver, the default name is Untitled Document, which is an even worse title for your page. Dreamweaver gives you several reminders if you haven't titled your page. Look at the document title bar. It contains the title and the file name. If you see "Untitled Document (filename.htm)," you haven't titled your document. You'll also see "Untitled Document" in the toolbar of the document window.*

SETTING DREAMWEAVER MX PREFERENCES

Once you are in Dreamweaver, you should designate Fireworks as the primary external image editor. This way, you can launch Fireworks to edit images while you are still in Dreamweaver. Most likely, this preference was set when you loaded both Fireworks MX and Dreamweaver MX, but it is easy to check.

1) In Dreamweaver, choose Edit > Preferences. In the Preferences dialog box, select File Types/Editors from the Category list.

FILE TYPES/EDITORS —

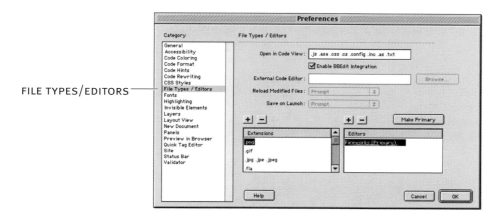

2) From the Extensions list, choose .png. If Fireworks doesn't appear in the Editors list, click the plus sign above the Editors list to find your Fireworks MX application. Select Fireworks from the Editors list. Then click Make Primary to make sure that Fireworks launches when you perform any edits. Repeat this process for the .gif and .jpg extensions in the Extensions list.

After you define the site and set the Dreamweaver preferences, you are ready to explore the integration between the two applications. You can also assign editors for other file types you might want to launch while in Dreamweaver. For example, you could add the .doc extension and assign Microsoft Word as the editor, or add the .fla extension and assign Macromedia Flash as the editor.

267

3) Select Preview in Browser from the Category list.

As you develop your Web pages, you will want to view your efforts in a browser—or, in fact, in several browsers. In Preferences, you can specify which browsers you want to use to preview your pages. To simplify the preview process, Dreamweaver has keyboard shortcuts for viewing your pages in two different browsers, referred to as the primary and secondary browsers.

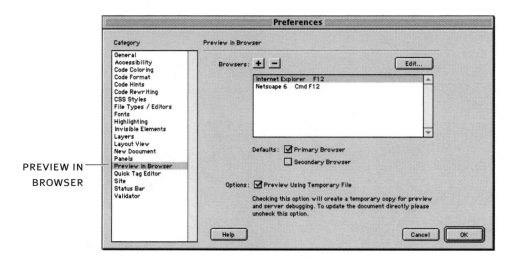

PREVIEW IN BROWSER

Do the following to select the browsers you want to use in previewing your pages:

- Click the plus (+) button to add a browser to the list. When the dialog box appears, find the browser application. Select Primary Browser if you want to launch this browser by pressing F12 when previewing your pages. Select Secondary Browser to preview your document by pressing Ctrl+F12 (Windows) or Command+F12 (Macintosh). You'll be using these shortcuts often, so memorize them quickly.

- To remove a browser from the list, select the browser name in the list and then click the minus (–) button.

- To change a browser choice, select the browser name in the list. Then click Edit and locate a different browser.

4) Click OK to close the Preferences dialog box.

VIEWING THE PAGE IN THE BROWSER

Once you have set your preferences, you can view your page in both the primary and secondary browsers. The quickest way is to use the keyboard shortcuts: F12 for the primary browser and Ctrl+F12 (Windows) or Command+F12 (Macintosh) for the secondary browser.

You can also click the globe button on the toolbar and select the browser from the pop-up menu. If you have several browsers defined, they will all appear in the menu.

GLOBE BUTTON

1) Use one of the methods described to view your page in the browser.

Move the pointer over the buttons and the month text to check your rollovers.

2) Click the About Us button and the Facts & Recipes button.

The links you assigned in Fireworks take you to the about.htm page and the facts.htm page. Clicking the other buttons results in an error message since you haven't created those pages.

You might notice that you have no way to return to the home page. In the next exercise, you will assign a link on your pages to return to your home page.

3) Close the browser and return to Dreamweaver.

ADDING LINKS

In Fireworks, you used the Property inspector to assign links to the slices. In Dreamweaver, you assign links to text or to an image on the page. You can use the Property inspector as you did in Fireworks, but you can also use the Site panel and simply point to the linked file.

1) Double-click the *about.htm* file on the Site panel. Title the page *About Us*.

On the About page, you see the text from the text slice.

2) Select the candy image.

You will use this image as the link to your home page.

3) Type *home_page.htm* in the Link text box of the Property inspector.

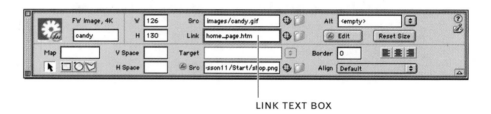

LINK TEXT BOX

The name you enter is the path name to the file as it relates to the current file. In this case, both the about.htm and home_page.htm files are located in the same folder, so you need to enter only the file name.

NOTE *If your home page has a different name, be sure to type that name instead.*

4) Save your file and then preview it in the browser. Click the candy to check that you are taken to the home page. Close the browser and return to Dreamweaver.

Typing the link in the Property inspector works fine, but if you make a spelling error in the name, the link won't work. In the next step, you will use the Site panel and point to the link file to enter its name.

5) Open the facts.htm file by double-clicking it on the Site panel. Title the page *Facts and Recipes*. Select the candy image on the page.

Look in the Property inspector to the right of the Link text box. You should see a circular icon and a folder icon. If you click the folder icon, you can browse to the file you want to use as the link. The circular icon—called Point-to-File—is what you use to point to the file on the Site panel.

> **TIP** *To use Point-to-File, you need to be able to see both your Document window and the files on the Site panel. You may need to move the windows so that they are side by side and not overlapping one another.*

6) Drag the Point-to-File icon to the home_page.htm file on the Site panel. Release the mouse button when you are over the file on the Site panel.

As you drag the icon, you'll see an arrow extend from it to help you place the link on the file. When you release the mouse button, the name of the file you pointed to is inserted in the Link text box. In this example, you could have just as easily typed the link as you did in step 3. The advantage of using the Point-to-File icon is revealed when you want to link to files that are within subfolders. For example, look at the text box labeled "Src" above the Link text box. The Src text box points to the location of the candy image. Since it is in the Images folder, its path name is images/candy.gif.

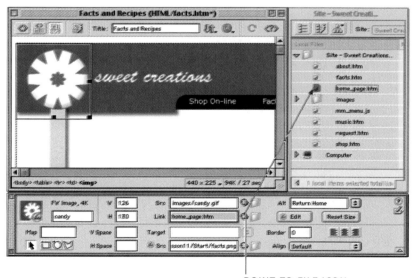

POINT-TO-FILE ICON

7) Save and then close your file.

271

OPTIMIZING IN FIREWORKS

While working in Dreamweaver, you may need to optimize a graphic you have placed on the page. You may have inherited a page from a co-worker with the image too large or not properly optimized.

1) Open the music.htm file in Dreamweaver and select the image of the guitar and CD.

The guitar and CD graphic is a large JPEG image that you defined in Lesson 5.

2) Right-click (Windows) or Control-click (Macintosh) the image and select Optimize in Fireworks from the contextual menu.

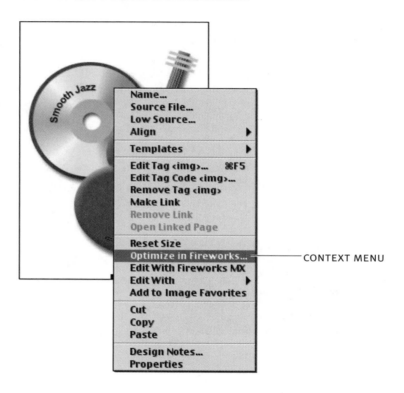

CONTEXT MENU

Fireworks opens, but in a special mode. In the Optimize Images dialog box, you can change the file format for images, the image quality for JPEG images, and the palette for GIF images. You'll see the image in the preview window as you change your settings.

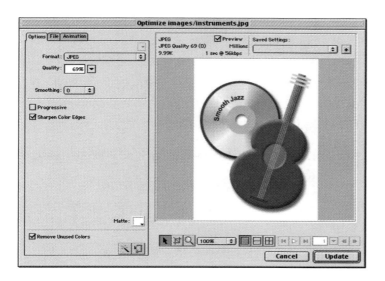

The Optimize Images dialog box is the same as the Export Preview dialog box in Fireworks. The difference is that in Dreamweaver you update the image, and in Fireworks you export the image. Export Preview is not covered in this book as it functions the same way as setting the optimization for your image and then choosing Export.

3) Move the Quality slider to decrease the JPEG quality slightly, until you see a change in the file size; then click Update.

Your image is re-exported with the new settings, and the image is updated within your page.

Normally, you should edit the source PNG file and then re-export your images. If you have received a page from a co-worker, however, you may not have the original source file. This exercise demonstrates the process of optimizing an image when you don't have the original source image.

4) Save and close this file.

EDITING IN FIREWORKS FROM DREAMWEAVER

When you create a page in Fireworks and then export it as HTML, Fireworks builds an HTML table the size of your canvas and creates cells within that table based on the slices or the slice guides. Once you are in Dreamweaver, you may want to return to Fireworks to make a change on the page. You could switch back to Fireworks, open the PNG file, export the file, and then return to Dreamweaver and open the new HTML page. Because of the integration of the two programs, however, the process is even easier. Just select the table on the HTML page and click once, and you are editing in Fireworks. Click once more, and the file is re-exported and you are returned to Dreamweaver. What could be easier?

1) Open the template.htm file by double-clicking it on the Site panel. Change the title to *Sweet Creations*.

This file contains the header, logo, and buttons that you've used at the top of all of the pages; there is also a large white image on the page. You will add a text slice in Fireworks to replace the image.

2) Click the white area in the middle of the page.

Look in the Property inspector to see the size of the image. It is a large image because you didn't draw any slices in this area. You could just delete this image in Dreamweaver and leave a large cell for inserting text or other images. Instead, you will edit this file in Fireworks and draw a smaller slice in this area, adding more white space around the cell.

The trick to editing the table that Fireworks created is to select that table in Dreamweaver. Look at the tag selector in the bottom left of the Document window. There you will see some HTML tags defining the page.

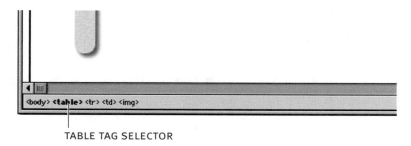

TABLE TAG SELECTOR

NOTE *If you see only the body tag, then click one of the images on the page. The other tags should appear.*

3) Click the ‹table› tag in the tag selector.

The table is selected, and the Property inspector changes to reflect the selection of a Fireworks table. You should see your Fireworks file listed in the Src text box.

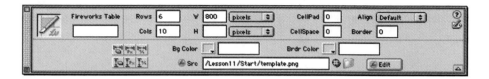

4) Click the Edit button.

The template.png file opens in Fireworks. At the top of the Document window, you'll see text indicating that you are editing from Dreamweaver; you'll also see a Done button.

5) Select the Slice tool and draw a slice within the white area of the canvas and then change the slice to an HTML slice.

Leave some space between the slice and the buttons and the slice of the stick. Extend the slice to the bottom of the canvas.

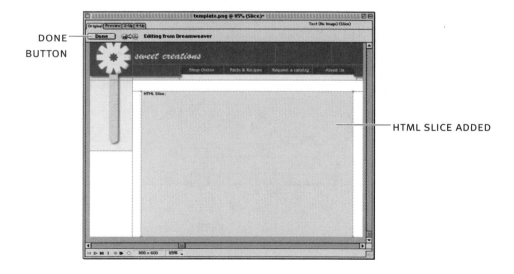

DONE BUTTON

HTML SLICE ADDED

6) Click Done.

Your file is saved, and you are returned to Dreamweaver. The page is updated with an empty cell where you drew the HTML slice. The title you added to the page is retained when you return to Dreamweaver.

CREATING A TEMPLATE IN DREAMWEAVER

In Fireworks, you created the template.png file and used that file as a starting point for the new files you created. That file contained the buttons and logo that you wanted to use on all of your pages. By creating new files from that file, you were able to create your new pages quickly and with the assurance that all of the buttons were the same.

In Dreamweaver, you can create a template that you can use to rapidly produce pages with the same design elements. You can define certain areas of the template as editable; all other areas then are locked and can't be edited. Locking areas ensures that the page design remains constant across all pages.

In this exercise, you will create a Dreamweaver template from the template.htm file you created in Fireworks. Then you will use that template to create recipe pages.

1) Open the template.htm page in Dreamweaver. Choose File > Save as Template.

The Save As Template dialog box opens. Here you see any existing templates for the site. The current site (Sweet Creations) is selected.

2) In the Save As text box, type *recipes* and then click Save.

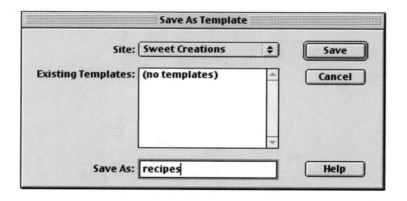

Your file is saved as a template. When you save a document as a template, Dreamweaver automatically inserts code that locks most regions of the document. You then need to identify the areas that you want to make editable. When you are editing the template, you have control over the entire document. When you are editing a page based on the template, you can modify only the editable regions of the document.

NOTE *Dreamweaver creates a Templates folder in your local site folder and saves your template file with a .dwt extension in the Templates folder.*

276

3) **Click within the large empty cell in the document and then choose Insert >**
Template Objects > Editable Region.

This area is defined as an HTML slice in Fireworks; you want to make it the
editable region of this template.

TIP *You can also right-click (Windows) or Control-click (Macintosh) and then choose*
Templates > New Editable Region from the context menu.

4) **Type *Content* in the Name text box of the New Editable Region dialog box and**
then click OK.

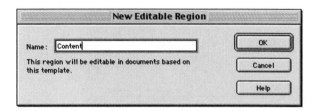

NOTE *The name you enter must be unique; you can't have the same name for multiple*
regions of a template. You also can't use quotation marks (single or double), angle brackets
(< >), or ampersands (&) in the name.

The region name is enclosed in a rectangle, and a tab in the upper left corner of the
region displays the region name.

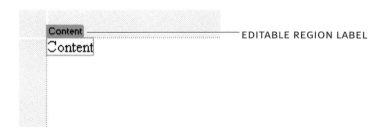

EDITABLE REGION LABEL

5) **Save and then close the template page.**

CREATING A TEMPLATE-BASED PAGE

You can now use the template to build new pages for your site.

1) Choose File > New. In the New Document dialog box, click the Templates tab.

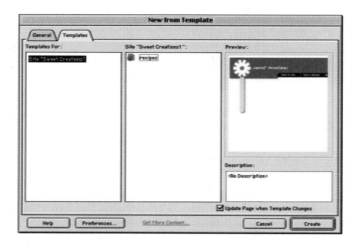

The left column displays your sites, the middle column displays a list of the templates for the selected site, and the right column displays a preview of the selected template.

2) Select the Sweet Creations site, select the Recipes template, and then click Create.

A new document based on your template opens. If you move your pointer over any of the buttons, the pointer changes to the universal No symbol to indicate that you can't modify the buttons in this area. The template name (recipes) appears at the top right of the document window to indicate that this document is based on a template.

UNIVERSAL NO SYMBOL

3) Change the title to *Mexican Hot Chocolate* and save the file as *hot_choc.htm* in the HTML folder within the Lessons folder.

In the editable region, you want to add the hot chocolate recipe.

ADDING TEXT IN DREAMWEAVER

Dreamweaver can open files created in word processing or page layout applications that have been saved as ASCII text files. For example, Dreamweaver can open a Microsoft Word document if you save the file as plain text or HTML. Text files (.txt files), as opposed to HTML files (.htm or .html files), open in Code view in Dreamweaver. After you open a text file in Dreamweaver, you can either copy and paste the text you need into another Dreamweaver file or save that file as a new HTML file. (A text file with the .txt extension will need the .htm or .html extension if you want the text file converted to an HTML file that opens in Dreamweaver.)

Simple document formatting such as paragraphs and line breaks can be retained, but you need to know a little about the differences in the ASCII format on the Windows and Macintosh platforms. Files created in Windows use an invisible control character called a line feed to indicate a new line within the text. Macintosh computers do not use the line-feed character. If you open a Windows text file in SimpleText on a Macintosh, you'll see a small rectangle at the beginning of each new paragraph, indicating the line-feed character. If you open a Macintosh text file in Windows, all of the paragraphs merge together because of the missing line-feed character.

Knowing this, you can change your preferences to match the file format of the text files you receive and want to open in Dreamweaver.

1) Choose Edit > Preferences and select Code Format from the Category list.

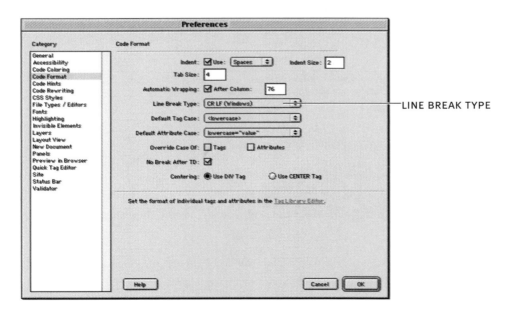

279

2) Select the option you need from the Line Break Type pop-up menu. Your choices here are CR LF (Windows), CR (Macintosh), and LF (Unix); choose the one that matches the text you are working with (not necessarily the one that matches your system). Click OK.

The text for this exercise was created in Windows. If you are using a Macintosh, change this setting to CR LF (Windows). If you are working in Windows, make sure you have the same setting.

3) Open the Lesson11 folder on the Site panel and then open the Text folder. Double-click the hot_choc.txt file in that folder.

The document opens in Code view.

4) Click the View Options button in the document window and then choose Word Wrap.

Word Wrap allows you to see all of the text in the instruction paragraph.

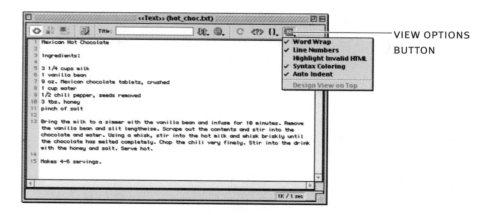

5) Select all of the text and then choose Edit > Copy.

You can close the text file.

6) In your hot_choc.htm file, click in the editable region and then choose Edit > Paste.

The hot chocolate recipe is inserted within the Content region. The recipe title (Mexican Hot Chocolate) is the first paragraph in the text.

> **NOTE** *If your text is not separated into paragraphs, then you didn't change your preferences to use CR LF (Windows) for the line breaks.*

7) Select the Mexican Hot Chocolate heading. In the Property inspector, choose Heading 3 from the Format pop-up menu.

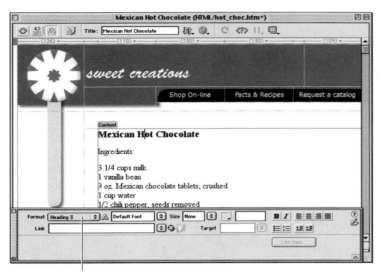

HEADING 3 IN PROPERTY INSPECTOR

HTML offers six heading tags that you can use to format your text. The heading format changes the text to bold and changes the size based on the heading number you choose. Heading 1 is the largest; Heading 6 is the smallest.

8) Save your page and preview it in the browser.

ON YOUR OWN

Create other recipe pages using the recipe template as you did in the preceding exercise. The Text folder contains several recipes that you can use to create your pages. For example, you can create cherry_choc.htm, choc_chip.htm, and so on. In the next exercise, you will modify the template and update all of the pages based on the template.

NOTE *When you preview your pages in the browser, you might notice that the candy stick moves down away from the candy. This happens because the text you inserted in the editable region is larger than the cell size in the region. The text expands the cell, causing the stick to move down. In the next exercise, you will modify the template to fix that problem.*

MODIFYING A TEMPLATE

One of the most powerful features of templates is the ability to update all of the template-based pages at once. You've seen how easy it is to create multiple pages based on the pages; in this exercise, you will modify the template and update all of the recipe pages.

To manage your templates, you use the Assets panel. Assets are a variety of elements you use in your site, such as images, Macromedia Flash movies, and templates.

1) Choose Window > Assets to open the Assets panel.

TEMPLATES ICON ON THE ASSETS PANEL

There are nine icons indicating the different categories of assets. When you roll over each icon, a tooltip appears to help you identify the category.

2) Click the Templates icon on the Assets panel.

The templates for your site appear in the Templates list.

3) Double-click the recipes template to open the template.

Be sure to double-click the icon to the left of the name. Double-clicking the name allows you to change the template name, but it doesn't open the template.

4) Select the candy stick image on the page. Press the left arrow key to move the insertion point into the table cell.

The image fills the entire table cell, and this method is a quick way to place the insertion point in the cell.

5) In the Property inspector, choose Top from the Vert pop-up menu.

The Vert pop-up menu controls the vertical alignment for objects in the cell. By changing the alignment to Top for the cell containing the stick, you force the image to move to the top of the cell. This keeps the stick aligned with the candy.

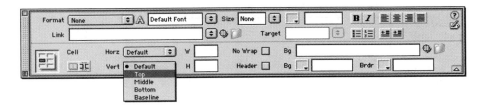

6) Save the template file.

The Update Template Files dialog box appears with a list of all of the files for your site that were created based on this template.

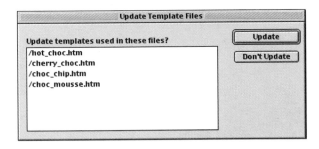

7) Click Update to update all of the pages with the link change.

A summary dialog box appears with the results of your updates. In this exercise, you had only a few pages to update. With multiple pages to update, you can see what a powerful feature this could be.

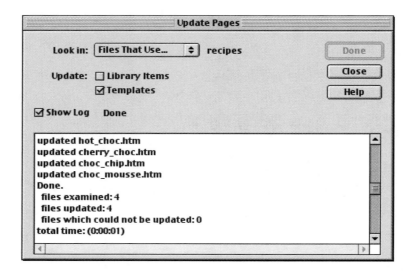

8) Click Close.

⊙ POWER TIP *All of the panels in Dreamweaver have an Options menu (as in Fireworks) located at the top right of the panel. On the Assets panel, you can choose New from Template from the Options menu. A new document is opened based on the selected template. This method is much quicker than choosing File > New and then selecting the Templates tab.*

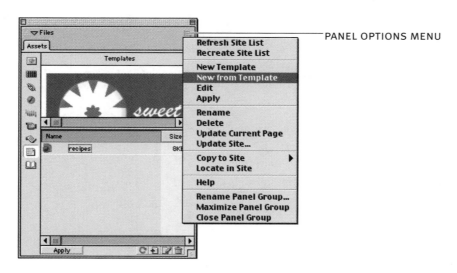

PANEL OPTIONS MENU

APPLYING A TEMPLATE TO A PAGE

In the preceding exercise, you created new pages based on the template you created. What if you have an existing document that you want to look like the other pages? You can select the elements on the page and then copy them into a new page you have created from the template. You can also apply the template to the existing page.

1) Open the request.htm file within the HTML folder.

This file contains a simple form for requesting a catalog.

2) On the Assets panel, select Templates and then click Apply.

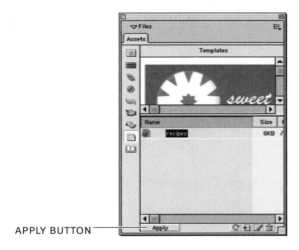

APPLY BUTTON

You want to apply the template to the open page. A dialog box opens informing you that your document contains inconsistent region names. Remember that you defined the center table cell of the template as an editable region named Content.

3) Select Document Body in the Inconsistent Region Names dialog box. In the Move Content to New Region pop-up menu, select Content. Click OK.

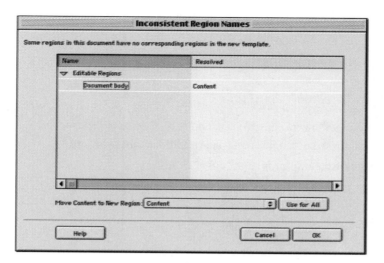

You are assigning the entire document to the Content region of the template. When you click OK, the template is applied to the file, and the form is contained within the center table cell.

4) Title the page *Request a Catalog* and then save your file.

MOVING FILES ON THE SITE PANEL

In Lesson 10, you created pop-up menus in Fireworks, adding text and links for the menus. Now in Dreamweaver, you've created some of the pages for those links. The file names for the recipe pages you just produced may not match the file names when you created the links in Fireworks. You can edit the pop-up menus in Dreamweaver and adjust the file names.

Before you edit the files, suppose you decide you want to organize them for the site. Currently, they are in the root folder of the site, along with the other pages you created. Instead, you want to store them in a separate folder within the site. This task is easily done on the Site panel.

1) Select the Lessons folder (the top folder) for your site. Right-click (Windows) or Control-click (Macintosh) and select New Folder from the context menu.

An untitled folder is added within the root folder, and the name (untitled) is selected.

2) Type *recipes* as the folder name; then press Enter (Windows) or Return (Macintosh). Drag the recipe files you created and drop them onto the recipe folder. Click Update.

When you move a file, Dreamweaver prompts you to update any file that links to that file.

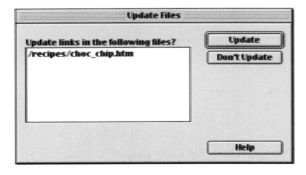

287

EDITING THE FIREWORKS POP-UP MENU

With the recipes files in a separate folder, you are now ready to edit the pop-up menus and change the links.

1) Open the facts.htm file on the Site panel and select the Chocolate Recipes button.

The image of the button contains the JavaScript for the pop-up menu. In Dreamweaver, as in Fireworks, predefined JavaScript code appears on the Behaviors panel. In Fireworks, you may have used the behavior handle on the slice to create the behavior. In Dreamweaver, you use the Behaviors panel.

2) Choose Window > Behaviors to open the Behaviors panel.

You should see a MouseOver event and a MouseOut event in the panel. When the user rolls over the image, the pop-up menu is displayed on the page. When the user rolls off the image, the pop-up menu is hidden.

3) Double-click the Show Pop-Up Menu action on the Behaviors panel.

The Show Pop-Up Menu dialog box is very similar to the one in Fireworks.

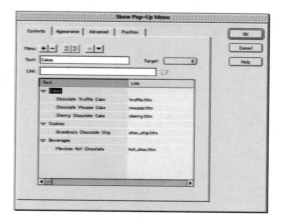

288

4) Select Mexican Hot Chocolate from the list. Click the folder icon to the right of the Link text field. Locate your hot_choc.htm file in the Recipes folder and then click Open.

The new path name for the link is added to the pop-up menu.

5) Repeat step 4 for the other recipe files you created. Click OK. Save your files and preview them in the browser.

Check the links in the pop-up menu to see that they work.

CONCLUSION

You made it. By working through the projects in this book, you should now have a good working knowledge of Fireworks. We hope you've been inspired with new ideas for adding visual interest to your Web pages. As you get more familiar with Fireworks, be sure to check the Macromedia Web page (www.macromedia.com) for updates and tips on using Fireworks.

WHAT YOU HAVE LEARNED

In this lesson, you have:

- Exported your pages as HTML for Dreamweaver [pages 257–258]
- Created a local site on your local disk for testing your HTML pages [pages 259–264]
- Viewed your HTML pages in Dreamweaver [pages 265–266]
- Set Dreamweaver preferences [pages 267–268]
- Viewed your HTML pages in the browser [pages 269]
- Added links to your pages in Dreamweaver [pages 270–271]
- Optimized an image in Fireworks from Dreamweaver [pages 272–273]
- Edited Fireworks files from Dreamweaver [pages 274–275]
- Created a Dreamweaver template and added text to a new page based on that template [pages 276–281]
- Modified the template and updated the pages [pages 282–284]
- Applied a template to a page [pages 285–286]
- Moved files on the Site panel [page 287]
- Edited the Fireworks pop-up menu in Dreamweaver [pages 288–289]

index

WWW.PEACHPIT.COM

Quality How-to Computer Books

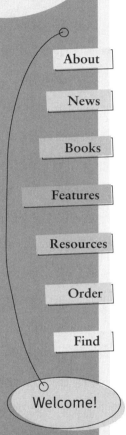

About

News

Books

Features

Resources

Order

Find

Welcome!

Visit Peachpit Press on the Web at www.peachpit.com

- Check out new feature articles each Monday: excerpts, interviews, tips, and plenty of how-tos

- Find any Peachpit book by title, series, author, or topic on the Books page

- See what our authors are up to on the News page: signings, chats, appearances, and more

- Meet the Peachpit staff and authors in the About section: bios, profiles, and candid shots

- Use Resources to reach our academic, sales, customer service, and tech support areas and find out how to become a Peachpit author

Peachpit.com is also the place to:

- Chat with our authors online
- Take advantage of special Web-only offers
- Get the latest info on new books